The London Coffee Guide. 2012

Edited by
Jeffrey Young
and Sally Conor

Author: Allegra Strategies
Photography: Maximilian Gower
& Warattaya S. Bullôt
Design: John Osborne
Website: Tim Spring
Publisher: Allegra Publications Ltd

Published in 2012 by Allegra Publications Ltd No.1 Northumberland Ave, Trafalgar Square, London, WC2N 5BW

Visit our website:
www.londoncoffeeguide.com

All information was accurate at time of going to press.

Published by *Allegra* PUBLICATIONS Ltd © 2012
No.1 Northumberland Ave, Trafalgar Square, London, WC2N 5BW

Foreword

As a Londoner with 100% Italian blood, I have a conflict that sits uneasily with me. Born in London, but with heritage from the country that invented espresso, I have to accept that the once unassailable position of the Italians as the coffee kings of London is now well and truly at an end, with the exception of a notable few. Those remaining, like the iconic Bar Italia in Frith Street, seem like bastions of the Italian way, built to defend against the tide of coffee bars whose talented, extremely knowledgeable, innovative and enthusiastic owners continue to push the boundaries and make London's coffee culture exciting, and unlike any other.

As an island nation, we have always absorbed other cultures easily, but seem to end up with something that is different and personal to us. This trait is epitomised within the London coffee scene. The ability to absorb, and a ready desire to accept something different, gives us the freedom to develop. Yes, Milan, Vienna, Sydney, New York and the rest have their scene, and their way of doing things, but London is unique in its diversity and its coffee culture is still evolving. This evolution is not all about espresso, as more wonderful coffees and different ways of brewing them are brought into the public domain. This break from the grip of espresso-dominated drinks is possible because of the passion of London's new coffee gurus and their desire to explore and share their knowledge with the public.

I would urge you to experiment and not to accept mediocrity. In London today there is no need to do so. It's not about the brand on the shop front, it's about the experience, and this guide will surely give you the chance to enjoy many new experiences.

Louie Salvoni
Managing director of
Espresso Service Ltd

Contents

Coffee passport	Inside front cover
Foreword	iii
Introduction	v
About the guide	vi
A brief history of London coffee shops	viii
Venue profiles:	
West End	1
West End & Soho map	2
Soho	27
Farringdon & Clerkenwell	47
Camden & Islington	59
Top 10 carts, stalls & kiosks	80
Inner East	87
Inner East map	89
Hackney	101
South East London	127
South West London	139
West London	151
Coffee glossary	158
A-Z list of coffee venues	163
Coffee map key	166
London coffee map	Inside back cover

Introduction

Welcome to The London Coffee Guide 2012 – the definitive guide to London's best coffee venues.

The London Coffee Guide was born out of a desire to find great places to go for coffee in London. These places used to be few and far between in the capital, but London is now home to a thriving independent coffee scene and both locals and visitors are spoilt for choice.

We have compiled The London Coffee Guide to assist and inform those who are keen to travel all over town in the hunt for great coffee venues. It might be the coffee itself that is the main attraction, or perhaps it's the excitement of visiting a new and unique coffee shop. Our aim is to encourage fellow coffee lovers to try something different and discover places they otherwise may never have known existed.

Allegra Strategies is a well-established leader in research and business intelligence to the coffee industry in the UK and Europe. It has drawn on this research as well as countless other sources (including industry experts, blogs, general community views and staff of the coffee venues themselves) to compile The London Coffee Guide.

About the Guide

Ratings

Every venue that appears in The London Coffee Guide has been visited and rated by our expert team. The ratings fall into two distinct categories: **coffee rating** and **overall rating**.

Coffee rating

The coffee rating is not only about the taste of the coffee - it also takes into account numerous other coffee credentials, such as the coffee roaster, equipment used, barista skills, visual appeal of the coffee and several other factors that demonstrate the venue's overall attitude to coffee. The following question is the guiding principle used to determine the coffee ratings:
To what extent does this coffee venue deliver an amazing coffee experience?

Overall rating

In combination with the coffee experience, the overall rating considers to what extent a coffee shop experience delivers a "wow" factor to the customer. Elements that are taken into account include: café environment, ambience, design, customer service and food quality. To determine a coffee shop's overall rating, the following question is used as the guiding principle: How does the combination of coffee and the coffee shop experience translate into exceptional levels of customer excitement?

The London Coffee Guide includes coffee carts, stalls and kiosks, as well as coffee shops. It was not considered fair to compare these venues with permanent cafés, so for 2012, these venues have not been given ratings. Instead, the ten best carts, stalls and kiosks and London have been grouped into a separate chapter (pp 80-85).

Symbols used throughout The London Coffee Guide

 Coffee beans sold on site

Decaffeinated coffee available

 Gluten-free products available

 Venue has a loyalty card

Soya milk available

 Toilets

 Parent & baby friendly

 Disabled access

 Wifi available

 Licensed

Peter Dore-Smith
Jeffrey Sheridan Young
Kenneth Cooper
Marc Dietrich
Kate Lewis
Glenn Bruce Watson
Steve Gotham
Anya Marco
Katarina Slezackova
Catherine Foley

Allegra would like to thank and congratulate the following **London Belle Barista team** and all the assistants on stand for achieving a **Guinness World record 12,003 espressos poured in a single hour by a team**

Adrienne Hruby
Alan Miller
Alberto Galimberti
Alena Simova
Alessandro Moretti
Amy Walker
Ania Chojnacka
Anna Kantorikova
Ariane Elaris
Arianna Pozzan
Ashleigh Hardway
Athanasios Athanatos
Ben Drury
Ben Hirons
Bernardo Sherwood
Camilla Runnquist
Carl Bjorkstrand
Carlos Machado
Charlie Mackenzie
Charlotte Holt
Chris Salierno
Christer Malmcrona
Christian Perez
Dacia McPherson
Dainoras Petrauskas
Dan Tanna
Daniel Clarke
Daniela Machado
David Craig
Don Eliezer Altizo
Egle Bagbonaite
Elliot Wallis
Enrico Wurm
Ermina Isanovic
Fabio Esposito
Filippo Silvestri
Franceso Sonapo
Francisco Silva
Frederik Rosenstand
Gabriela Machado
Gary Diggett
Gavin Firnback
Gennaro Aniello
Giovanni Altieri
Giovanni Gervasio
Gustavo Gallardo
Haddon Rustin
Halina Klos
Hazel Burns
Henry Ayers
Howard Barwick
Isaac Khurgel
Isabela Machado
Ishaq Kazi
James Wakelin
James Connery
James Fisher
James Tateo
Jamie Nulph
Jenna Montgomery
Jeremy Torz
Joanna Polak
Joanna Szonert
Joao Almeida
Jochem Verheijen
Jon Cowell
Kristina Melankite
Kristina Petrauskaite
Krysty Prasolik
Leo Tong
Lorenzo Carboni
Mahabub Alam
Marc Berkovi
Margus Varvas
Mariusz Lewicki
Martha Crouch
Matteo Capobianco
Matthew Tuffee
Melissa Mace
Micah Steinwandt
Mike Sugrue
Monika Simion
Myra Sheehan
Nadine Jojo
Natalia Toronska
Nick Payne
Nicolas Pasquali
Niomi Taylor
Olivier Meurou
Olivier Vetter
Pam Kaur
Paul Eagles
Paul Kelly
Phil Sung
Philip Lowe
Riccardo Dumi
Richard Thomas
Rikki Fairgold
Robert Henry
Robert Ward
Rodolfo Magalhaes
Rummy Keshet
Sally Chapman
Sam Dunford
Sean Pittaway
Sivaraj Thamichelvam
Steve Fernandes
Stuart Summers
Syfyl Islam
Tim Sturk
Toana Adrian Dumitru
Tom Handiside
Tomas Bruckus
Vered Berkovi
Will Corby
William Laycock

A Brief History of London Coffee Shops

The early years

800 AD The coffee plant (Coffea) attracts human interest and consumption as early as 800 AD in the Kaffe region of Ethiopia. According to legend, it was an Ethiopian goat herder named Kaldi who first discovered how animated his herd of goats became after chewing on the red berries.

Mid 17th century

Travellers to Middle Eastern areas such as the Ottoman Empire bring coffee to Europe and Britain.

1650 The first English coffee house is established in Oxford by a Jewish gentleman named Jacob at the Angel in the parish of St Peter.

Coffee houses become meeting places for political and literary debates between artists, intellectuals, merchants and bankers. Such venues are known as Penny Universities, in reference to the one penny entrance fee. They are closely associated with reading and provide pamphlets and newspapers, as well as copious amounts of coffee.

1652 London's first coffee house is established by Pasqua Rosée in St Michael's Alley, Cornhill, London EC3.

1668 Edward Lloyd's Coffee House in Lombard Street becomes a key meeting place for ship owners and marine insurance brokers. Situated on the site occupied by Lloyds bank today, this coffee house likely contributed to London becoming a global hub for insurance and financial services.

1674 The Women's Petition Against Coffee is set up in London in response to men spending less time at home due to the "excessive use of the drying and enfeebling liquor".

1675 There are now more than 3,000 coffee houses across England. King Charles II attempts to outlaw coffee houses as hotbeds of revolution, but following large public protests, his proclamation is revoked after 11 days.

1680 Jonathan's Coffee House is established by Jonathan Miles in Change Alley. It is a place where stockbrokers frequently meet and eventually becomes today's London Stock Exchange.

1706 Thomas Twining opens the first known tea room in London, which can still be found at 216 Strand.

18th century

Coffee houses gradually decline in popularity and become more elite establishments, when they start charging more than one penny for entrance. Travelling taverns replace coffee houses as popular social spaces. Coffee also becomes a less important commodity as the East India Company and British trade in general focuses more on tea imports from India.

Last century

1894 Lyons opens a chain of tea rooms followed by Lyons Corner Houses in London's West End in 1906.

1923 The Kenya Coffee Company Limited (Kenco) is established and soon begins selling coffee on Vere Street, Mayfair.

1950s Italian-run espresso houses featuring Formica-topped tables are a popular feature of this era, particularly in London's Soho.

1952 Moka Bar opens on Frith Street and is London's first espresso bar.

1971 Starbucks opens its first store at Pike Place Market in Seattle, USA.

First Costa Coffee shop opened by brothers Sergio and Bruno Costa at 9 Newport Street, London.

1978 An early pioneer of artisanal coffee, Monmouth Coffee Company opens in Monmouth Street, Covent Garden.

1986 Pret A Manger is established by college friends Julian Metcalf and Sinclair Beecham.

1992 Fairtrade Foundation is established in London by the Catholic Overseas Development Agency, Christian Aid, Oxfam, Traidcraft and the World Development Movement, and is soon followed by the Women's Institute.

1995 Whitbread Group acquires Costa Coffee with 41 stores and a roastery in Lambeth.

1997 Nescafé opens first Café Nescafé trial stores in London and UK, but closes all outlets several years later.

Gerry Ford acquires five Caffè Nero stores and begins building a chain, which grows to become the third-largest coffee shop brand in the UK.

1998 Starbucks launches in the UK, acquiring 65 Seattle Coffee Company stores for an estimated £52 million.

1999 Allegra Strategies releases the groundbreaking Project Café Report, which predicts a significant boom in coffee shops.

Last decade

2000 Internet cafés grow in popularity during the dotcom era.

Marks & Spencer launches Café Revive concept.

2001 The caffé latte is added to the Consumer Price Index (CPI), the basket of goods the government uses to measure products purchased by a typical British household.

2006 The number of branded chain coffee shop outlets exceeds 1,000 in London alone.

2007 Flat White coffee shop opens in Berwick Street, Soho, setting the stage for further Antipodean influences on coffee in the UK.

James Hoffmann is crowned World Barista Champion and founds Square Mile Coffee Roasters.

2008 The first-ever European Coffee Symposium is held at London's Park Lane Hotel.

2009 A host of new artisanal "third wave" coffee shops open in London.

The UK's Gwilym Davies is crowned World Barista Champion.

2010 Costa, Starbucks and several other mainstream coffee chains launch their versions of the flat white.

The World Barista Championships are held in London at Caffè Culture.

The first edition of the London Coffee Guide is published.

2011 Growth of artisanal coffee shops and micro coffee roasteries in London continues to accelerate in 2011 with the arrival of St. Ali, Sensory Lab and Prufrock Coffee.

First-ever London Coffee Festival held at the Old Truman Brewery on Brick Lane.

West End

London's West End is synonymous with the city's legendary theatre and music scene, as well as its restaurants, shopping and nightlife. Business people and actors rub shoulders with tourists and urbanites, and the area's café culture is just as diverse.

COFFEE VENUES KEY

West End

1 **The Borough Barista** p4
2 **Caffè Nero** Bedford Street p5
3 **Costa Coffee** Great Portland Street p6
4 **Fernandez & Wells** Somerset House p7
5 **Joe & The Juice** Regent Street p8
6 **Kaffeine** p10
7 **Lantana** p12
8 **Monmouth Coffee Company** Covent Garden p14
9 **New Row Coffee** p15
10 **Notes, Music & Coffee** Wellington Street p16
11 **Patisserie Valerie** Marylebone p17
12 **The Providores & Tapa Room** p18
13 **Reynolds** Charlotte Street p19
14 **Sensory Lab** p20
15 **Store Street Espresso** p22
16 **Tapped & Packed** Rathbone Place p24
17 **Tapped & Packed** Tottenham Court Road p25

A **The 3 Little Pigs** at Black Truffle (Kiosk) p80

Soho

18 Bar Italia p28
19 Fernandez & Wells Beak Street p30
20 Flat White p32
21 Foxcroft & Ginger p34
22 Milkbar p35
23 Nordic Bakery p36
24 Nude Espresso Soho Square p38
25 Princi p40
26 Sacred Ganton Street p41
27 Speakeasy p42
28 Starbucks Conduit Street p44

The Borough Barista

60 Seymour Street, W1H 7JN

OPEN.

Mon-Fri. 7:30am - 5:00pm
Sat-Sun. 10:00am - 5:00pm

Tim Bloxsome describes his new Borough Barista concept as a British coffee bar with a "cleaner edge" than its high street chain-store rivals. By delivering delicious British food and beautifully prepared - but not intimidating - coffee to his customers, Bloxsome hopes to bring something new and fresh to the London coffee scene. This venue on Seymour Street not only provides a calm oasis of blonde wood and friendly service just around the corner from Marble Arch, but will soon offer coffee making and appreciation classes for keen customers.

FOOD.

Locally made and sourced sandwiches, pastries and cakes.

CONTACT.

+44(0)20 7563 7222
www.theboroughbarista.com
Marble Arch

OVERVIEW.

Category
Artisanal Independent
Owner
Tim Bloxsome and David Adam
First opened
November 2011

COFFEE & EQUIPMENT.

Coffee roaster
Union Hand-Roasted
Coffee machine
Rebuilt La Marzocco Linea, 3 groups
Coffee grinder
San Remo, Mazzer Jolly, Europa

COFFEE PRICING.

Espresso	£1.70 / £1.90
Cappuccino	£2.40 / £2.80
Latte	£2.40 / £2.80
Flat white	£2.40 / £2.80

RATING.

COFFEE 4.25 / 5

OVERALL 4.25 / 5

Caffè Nero Bedford Street

10 Bedford Street, WC2E 7HE

OPEN.

Mon-Fri.	6:30am - 9:00pm
Sat.	7:30am - 9:00pm
Sun.	8:30am - 8:00pm

This Caffè Nero store, located inside a stately old building on a busy corner in the middle of Charing Cross and Covent Garden, is a convenient stop for tourists on the well-trodden path around the West End. The simple interior, with its wooden furnishings and high ceilings, provides a comfortable place to relax and enjoy the Caffé Nero traditional Italian coffee experience.

FOOD.

Iced drinks, sandwiches, soups, pastas, salads, cakes, muffins, biscuits and pastries.

CONTACT.

+44(0)20 7240 9399
www.caffenero.com
enquiries@caffenero.com
Leicester Square

Sister coffee shops.
Over 400 UK outlets

OVERVIEW.

Category
Chain
Owner
Caffè Nero Group Ltd
First opened
2002

COFFEE & EQUIPMENT.

Coffee roaster
Caffè Nero
Coffee machine
Faema E91 Ambassador, 4 groups
Coffee grinder
Mazzer Super Jolly

COFFEE PRICING.

Espresso	£1.40 / £1.50
Cappuccino	£1.80 / £2.20 / £2.50
Latte	£1.80 / £2.20 / £2.50

RATING.

COFFEE
3.75 / 5

OVERALL
4.00 / 5

Costa Coffee Great Portland Street

4 Great Portland Street, W1W 8QJ

Image supplied by Costa Coffee

OPEN.

Mon-Fri.	6:30am - 10:00pm
Sat.	7:30am - 10:00pm
Sun.	8:30am - 8:00pm

This Costa Coffee store is a departure from the chain's usual branding and decor. Its interior is modern and stylish with painted brick, distressed wood and a feature wall of brightly coloured flowers. Seating is a combination of benches, communal and private tables, and a secluded nook in the corner is almost always occupied. Just a stone's throw from Oxford Circus, this Costa is a welcome retreat for weary shoppers.

FOOD.

Costa Coffee sandwiches, cakes, muffins and cookies.

CONTACT.

+44(0)20 7436 7325
www.costa.co.uk
customer.relations@whitbread.com
Oxford Circus

Sister coffee shops.
Over 1000 in the UK

OVERVIEW.

Category
Chain
Owner
Whitbread PLC
First opened
2010

COFFEE & EQUIPMENT.

Coffee roaster
Costa Coffee
Coffee machine
Costa Coffee Marisa, 3 groups x 2
Coffee grinder
Mazzer

COFFEE PRICING.

Espresso	£1.35 / £1.70
Cappuccino	£2.05 / £2.35 / £2.55
Latte	£2.05 / £2.35 / £2.55
Flat white	£2.25

RATING.

Fernandez & Wells Somerset House

Somerset House, Strand, WC2R 1LA

OPEN.

Mon-Fri.	8:00am - 11:00pm
Sat.	10:00am - 11:00pm
Sun.	10:00am - 10:00pm

This new venue from Fernandez & Wells occupies three rooms in one of London's most beautiful buildings and is an exercise in providing customers with the very best of everything: Sicilian panettone, Amalfi lemons, the finest meats, cheeses and wines, artisanal Lithuanian hot chocolate ... the list goes on. Coffee is at the heart of this experience, with a skilled crew of baristas pulling superb espresso from a pair of Synesso Cyncras, as well as preparing a range of single-estate filter coffees. This is more than a café - it's a fine food and coffee emporium.

FOOD.

Freshly prepared sandwiches, cakes and pastries, plus a range of fine delicatessen foods and a delicious brunch menu.

CONTACT.

www.fernandezandwells.com
taste@fernandezandwells.com
Temple

OVERVIEW.

Category
Eatery
Owner
Jorge Fernandez and Rick Wells
First opened
November 2011

COFFEE & EQUIPMENT.

Coffee roaster
Has Bean Coffee
Coffee machine
Synesso Cyncra, 3 groups x 2
Coffee grinder
Mazzer

COFFEE PRICING.

Espresso	£2.30
Latte	£2.60

Sister coffee shops.
Beak Street / Lexington Street / St. Anne's Court

RATING.

COFFEE 4.25 / 5

OVERALL 4.50 / 5

Joe & the Juice Regent Street

281 Regent Street, W1B 2HE

This flagship venue for well-established Danish chain Joe & the Juice is an entertaining destination that combines an extensive coffee menu with a range of delicious fresh juices and healthy lunch options. The charming staff, comfy sofas and large upstairs lounge-style area make this a vibrant West End location that is always alive with the chatter and excitement of the city. Joe & the Juice will open a new Soho venue in 2012 to complement its existing Broadwick Street location.

Sister coffee shops.
Broadwick Street / King's Road / Dean Street / 25 in Denmark / 1 in Sweden

COFFEE OVERLOAD 3 SHOTS +35p
ESPRESSO 1.55
DOUBLE ESPRESSO 1.90
MACCHIATO 2.05
CAPPUCCINO 2.50
CUP OF JOE 1.80
"TURKEY" 4.25
"TUNACADO" 4.45
"JOE'S CLUB" 4.45
All of JOE'S sandwiches are made with our own homemade pesto!
EXTRA TOPPING +50p

OPEN.

Mon-Fri.	7:30am - 9:00pm
Sat.	9:00am - 8:00pm
Sun.	10:00am - 8:00pm

OVERVIEW.

Category
Chain
Owner
Morten Basse and
Joe & The Juice RS Ltd
Head barista
Oliver Rechnitzer
First opened
2009

COFFEE & EQUIPMENT.

Coffee roaster
Vida e Caffé
Coffee machine
La Marzocco GB/5
Coffee grinder
Mazzer

COFFEE PRICING.

Espresso	£1.55
Cappuccino	£2.40
Latte	£1.90 / £2.10 / £2.30 / £2.60
Flat white	£2.30

FOOD.

A tempting selection of fresh and colourful homemade paninis, sandwiches and juices made to order.

CONTACT.

www.joejuice.com
morty@joejuice.com
Oxford Circus

RATING.

COFFEE
4.00 / 5

OVERALL
4.25 / 5

Kaffeine

66 Great Titchfield Street, W1W 7QJ

Since opening in 2009, Kaffeine has established itself as one of London's preeminent coffee venues. Owner Peter Dore-Smith sets the bar high and his team strives to provide the best café experience possible for allcomers, from casual lunch customers to coffee experts. Kaffeine is distinguished by its impeccable attention to detail, from the stylish wooden interior to the fresh food on offer and the precise latte art on each carefully crafted coffee. It's easy to see why this Fitzrovian favourite has developed such a loyal following and why it won Best Independent Coffee Shop in Europe for 2010.

OPEN.

Mon-Fri.	7:30am - 6:00pm
Sat.	9:00am - 6:00pm
Sun.	9:30am - 5:00pm

OVERVIEW.

Category
Artisanal Independent
Owner
Peter Dore-Smith
Head barista
James Broadhurst
First opened
2009

COFFEE & EQUIPMENT.

Coffee roaster
Square Mile Coffee Roasters
Coffee machine
Synesso Cyncra, 3 groups
Coffee grinder
Mazzer Robur E, Anfim

COFFEE PRICING.

Espresso	£1.60 / £2.10
Cappuccino	£2.50
Latte	£2.50
Flat white	£2.40

FOOD.

Fresh salads, focaccias, baguettes, pastries, soups and cookies, all freshly made on site.

CONTACT.

+44(0)20 7580 6755
www.kaffeine.co.uk
peter@kaffeine.co.uk
Oxford Circus, Goodge Street

RATING.

COFFEE 4.50 / 5

OVERALL 4.50 / 5

Lantana

13 Charlotte Place, W1T 1SN

Stylish and modern Fitzrovia favourite Lantana has gone from strength to strength since opening in 2008. This café and eatery is always abuzz with chatter and filled with loyal patrons, particularly during the weekend when its legendary brunch menu has customers queuing out the door. The coffee here is of a consistently high quality, both on the main premises and at the second shop next door that caters just for takeaway traffic.

Sister coffee shops.

Lantana Out (next door)

TOP 30

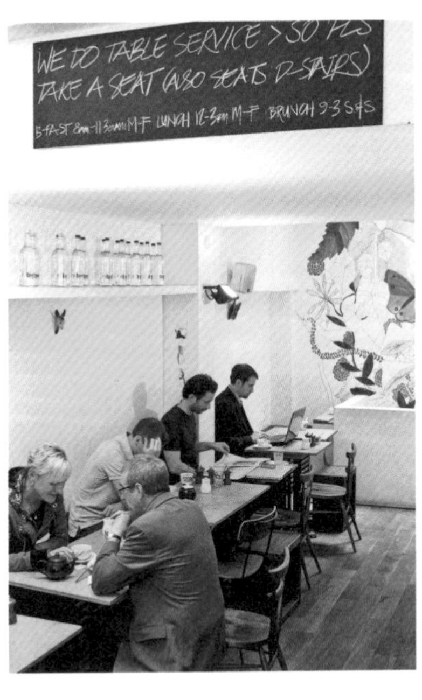

OPEN.

Mon-Fri. 8.00am - 6.00pm
Sat-Sun. 9:00am - 5:00pm

OVERVIEW.

Category
Artisanal Independent

Owner
Shelagh Ryan

First opened
2008

COFFEE & EQUIPMENT.

Coffee roaster
Square Mile Coffee Roasters

Coffee machine
La Marzocco Linea, 3 groups

Coffee grinder
Anfim, Mazzer Super Jolly

COFFEE PRICING.

Espresso	£1.60 / £1.80
Cappuccino	£2.50
Latte	£2.50
Flat white	£2.50

FOOD.

An appealing range of fresh and healthy salads, sandwiches and soups follow on from the breakfast menu. The weekend brunch menu is one of the best in London.

CONTACT.

+44(0)20 7637 3347
www.lantanacafe.co.uk
shelagh.ryan@gmail.com
Goodge Street

RATING.

COFFEE 4.50 / 5

OVERALL 4.50 / 5

TOP 30

Monmouth Coffee Company Covent Gdn

27 Monmouth Street, WC2H 9EU

This is where the Monmouth phenomenon began, back in 1978. The original Monmouth roastery occupied this site until 2007 when it moved to Bermondsey and the revamped interior here focuses attention entirely on the coffee. Wooden booths encourage strangers to share space and a chat, and mobile phone use is banned. Monmouth Coffee is nothing short of exceptional, as a busy team of baristas pull each shot with expert care. More often than not, queues of people snake out the door onto the pavement, but it's definitely worth the wait.

FOOD.

A selection of pastries, croissants, cakes and tarts are displayed on the counter by the entrance.

CONTACT.

+44(0)20 7379 3516
www.monmouthcoffee.co.uk
beans@monmouthcoffee.co.uk
Covent Garden

OPEN.

Mon-Sat. 8:00am - 6:30pm
Sun. Closed

OVERVIEW.

Category
Artisanal Independent
Owner
Anita Le Roy
First opened
1978

COFFEE & EQUIPMENT.

Coffee roaster
Monmouth Coffee Company
Coffee machine
La Marzocco Linea, 3 groups
Coffee grinder
Mazzer

COFFEE PRICING.

Espresso	£1.35
Cappuccino	£2.35
Latte	£2.35
Flat white	£2.35

Sister coffee shops.
The Borough / Bermondsey

Also serves **single-origin filter coffee**. Coffee is roasted at Monmouth Coffee Company roastery in Bermondsey

New Row Coffee

24 New Row, WC2N 4LA

OPEN.

Mon-Thu.	7:30am - 7:00pm
Fri.	7:30am - 8:00pm
Sat.	9:00am - 8:00pm
Sun.	9:00am - 6:00pm

This miniature coffee house is staffed by a crack team of coffee obsessives who discuss latte art in their downtime and prepare the best flat white on a street crammed with chain outlets. Daily drip pourover options are available at the bar, along with an enticing lemon drizzle cake, gourmet cookies and a range of pastries and sandwiches. Fresh almond milk is prepared each day - try it for a twist on your usual coffee of choice.

FOOD.

Tasty cakes, pastries, giant biscuits and muffins from local suppliers. Breakfast granola is available to buy.

CONTACT.

+44(0)20 3583 6949

Leicester Square

OVERVIEW.

Category
Artisanal Independent

Owner
Tom Cummings

First opened
October 2011

COFFEE & EQUIPMENT.

Coffee roaster
Union Hand-Roasted

Coffee machine
La Marzocco, 3 groups

Coffee grinder
Mazzer Luigi

COFFEE PRICING.

Espresso	£1.60
Cappuccino	£2.50
Latte	£2.50
Flat white	£2.40

RATING.

COFFEE 4.25 / 5

OVERALL 4.00 / 5

TOP 30

Notes, Music & Coffee Wellington St

36 Wellington Street, WC2E 7BD

OPEN.

Mon-Fri.	8:00am - 11:00pm
Sat.	9:00am - 11:00pm
Sun.	10:00am - 7:30pm

Just a stone's throw from the Royal Opera House, this venue is the perfect place for lovers of the arts to browse racks of music and films, or enjoy a delicious homemade pastry. Lovers of coffee, however, come here for the menu that includes Square Mile espresso, Has Bean single-origin espressos and a range of filter coffees sourced from roasteries across Europe that are brewed using only the highest-quality water. Tasting evenings for coffee, wine and whisky are also held for those who want to learn more.

FOOD.

Homemade pies, gourmet sausage rolls, sandwiches, cakes and salads. Charcuterie and fine cheeses are also available for purchase.

CONTACT.

+44(0)20 7240 7899
notesmusiccoffee.com
notescoventgdn@gmail.com
Covent Garden

Sister coffee shops.
Notes (St Martin's Lane)

OVERVIEW.

Category
Artisanal Independent
Owner / Head barista
Fabio Ferreira
First opened
September 2011

COFFEE & EQUIPMENT.

Coffee roaster
Square Mile Coffee Roasters
Coffee machine
La Marzocco Strada, 3 groups
Coffee grinder
Mazzer Robur E, Anfim

COFFEE.

Espresso	£1.80 / £2.20
Cappuccino	£2.60
Latte	£2.60
Flat white	£2.60

RATING.

COFFEE 4.50 / 5

OVERALL 4.25 / 5

Patisserie Valerie Marylebone

105 Marylebone High Street, W1U 4RS

OPEN.

Mon-Fri.	7:30am - 7:00pm
Sat.	8:00am - 7:00pm
Sun.	8:30am - 6:00pm

This Patisserie Valerie store is something of a Marylebone instution. Inside, the Palladian murals that adorn the walls transport customers to the continental Europe of the 1920s. Plenty of delectable sweet treats are available to enjoy with an Illy coffee, or something heartier from the all-day breakfast menu is equally satisfying.

FOOD.

Famous for its French patisserie cakes, croissants and treats, also serves continental breakfast, brunch and specialty sandwiches.

CONTACT.

+44(0)20 7935 6240
www.patisserie-valerie.co.uk
marylebone@valeriecafe.co.uk
Baker Street

Sister coffee shops.
50+ UK locations

OVERVIEW.

Category
Chain
Owner
Patisserie Holdings Ltd
First opened
1993

COFFEE & EQUIPMENT.

Coffee roaster
Illy
Coffee machine
Fracino, 3 groups
Coffee grinder
Mazzer srl Super Jolly

COFFEE PRICING.

Espresso	£1.80 / £2.70
Cappuccino	£2.80
Latte	£2.80

RATING.

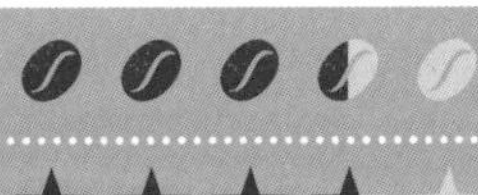

The Providores & Tapa Room

109 Marylebone High Street, W1U 4RX

OPEN.

Mon-Fri.	9:00am - 11:00pm
Sat.	10:00am - 11:00pm
Sun.	10:00am - 10:30pm

Run by New Zealand chef Peter Gordon, The Providores is a fusion eatery on upmarket Marylebone High Street that offers a range of innovative food and drink with a South Pacific flavour. The venue's ground-floor Tapa Room features a huge Rarotongan tapa cloth on one wall and heaves with people from breakfast to dinner, while the dining room upstairs caters for a more formal lunch and dinner crowd. Coffee is supplied by up-and-coming London roastery Volcano Coffee Works and is the perfect accompaniment to a delicious brunch at this popular venue.

FOOD.

A fusion breakfast menu, tapas for sharing and more substantial mains.

CONTACT.

+44(0)20 7935 6175
www.theprovidores.co.uk
anyone@theprovidores.co.uk
Baker Street

OVERVIEW.

Category
Eatery
Owner
Peter Gordon and Michael McGrath
Head barista
Melanie Ellis
First opened
2001

COFFEE & EQUIPMENT.

Coffee roaster
Volcano Coffee Works
Coffee machine
La Marzocco GB/5, 2 groups
Coffee grinder
Mazzer Super Jolly

COFFEE PRICING.

Espresso	£2.00 / £2.40
Cappuccino	£2.80
Latte	£2.80
Flat white	£2.80

RATING.

COFFEE
4.25 / 5

OVERALL
4.25 / 5

Reynolds Charlotte Street

53 Charlotte Street, W1T 4PA

OPEN.

Mon-Fri. 7:30am - 5:00pm
Sat-Sun. Closed

Reynolds is a fresh and upbeat eatery and coffee shop in London's West End. The owners are strong believers in reuse and recycling - the back wall is made of old packing crates, the lights are salvaged from an old factory and regular customers are rewarded for reusing their takeaway paper bags and coffee sleeves. The space is welcoming and communal, and art exhibitions on the walls rotate monthly to keep things interesting.

FOOD.

A grazing menu featuring smaller portions of wraps, sandwiches and salads - share with friends or try a few for yourself.

CONTACT.

+44(0)20 7580 0730
www.letsgrazereynolds.co.uk
hello@letsgrazereynolds.co.uk
Goodge Street

Sister coffee shops.
Eastcastle Street

OVERVIEW.

Category
Eatery
Owner
Ben Reynolds
First opened
2009

COFFEE & EQUIPMENT.

Coffee roaster
Union Hand-Roasted
Coffee machine
Nuova Simonelli Aurelia, 2 groups
Coffee grinder
Mazzer Super Jolly

COFFEE PRICING.

Espresso	£1.60
Cappuccino	£2.10
Latte	£2.10
Flat white	£2.10

RATING.

COFFEE 4.00 / 5

OVERALL 4.00 / 5

Sensory Lab

75 Wigmore Street, W1U 1QD

At Sensory Lab, great coffee is a science and its baristas are laureates of the highest order. This is coffee at its best, brewed with clinical precision and minute attention to detail: you'll be hard pressed to find more symmetrical latte art anywhere in London. This new location under the St. Ali umbrella is the first in an ambitious expansion plan that includes a new Marylebone location and more to follow. This location provides the blueprint, with a sleek and minimal marble and dark wood interior, simple bar-style seating, a small range of pastries enshrined behind polished glass and a range of St. Ali beans and coffee-making equipment available to buy. The brewing station offers a weekly programme of single-origin coffees, making Sensory Lab the complete coffee research destination.

OPEN.

Mon-Fri. 7:00am - 5:00pm
Sat-Sun. 10:00am - 5:00pm

OVERVIEW.

Category
Artisanal Independent
Owner
Charles and James Dickson
Head barista
Baptiste Kreyder
First opened
August 2011

COFFEE & EQUIPMENT.

Coffee roaster
St. Ali
Coffee machine
Synesso Cyncra, 3 groups
Coffee grinder
Mazzer

Sister coffee shops.
St. Ali

COFFEE PRICING.

Espresso	£2.00
Cappuccino	£2.40
Latte	£2.60
Flat white	£2.40

FOOD.

A small range of pastries and muffins.

CONTACT.

www.sensory-lab.co.uk
info@sensory-lab.co.uk
Bond Street

RATING.

COFFEE 4.50 / 5

OVERALL 4.50 / 5

Store Street Espresso

40 Store Street, WC1E 7DB

This exciting venue joined the burgeoning foodie scene on Store Street in 2010 and crowds of hungry students and young creatives have been flocking here ever since for the great coffee and electric atmosphere. The café itself is stylish and light-filled, with an ambience that encourages customers to linger for leisure, study or work. A passionate team of baristas serves Square Mile coffee accompanied by a youthful soundtrack that perfectly complements the buzz of the excellent flat whites.

TOP 30

West End

OPEN.

Mon-Fri.	7:30am - 7:00pm
Sat.	9:00am - 6:00pm
Sun.	9:00am - 5:00pm

OVERVIEW.

Category
Artisanal Independent
Owner
Roger Hart and Jack Hesketh
Head barista
Chris Weaver
First opened
2010

COFFEE & EQUIPMENT.

Coffee roaster
Square Mile Coffee Roasters
Coffee machine
La Marzocco Linea, 2 groups
Coffee grinder
Anfim

COFFEE PRICING.

Espresso	£1.60 / £1.80
Cappuccino	£2.30
Latte	£2.30
Flat white	£2.30

FOOD.

Fresh sandwiches, baguettes and salads, delicious cookies and cakes.

Single-origin espresso and **pourover options** also available

CONTACT.

www.storestreetespresso.com
storestreetespresso@gmail.com
Goodge Street

RATING.

COFFEE 4.25 / 5

OVERALL 4.25 / 5

West End

TOP 30

Tapped & Packed Rathbone Place

26 Rathbone Place, W1T 1JD

London coffee haven Tapped & Packed was one of the first to offer a selection of espresso blends, as well as an ever-changing menu of brewed coffee from artisanal roasters. Customers can select their coffee of choice and preferred brewing method (filter, cafetiere, or AeroPress) or ask the knowledgeable baristas for help to decide. A fantastic place to learn about the artistry of coffee, Tapped & Packed is one of London's best coffee destinations.

FOOD.

Gourmet breakfast, all-day pastries, cakes and chocolates.

CONTACT.

+44(0)20 7580 2163
www.tappedandpacked.co.uk
postmaster@tappedandpacked.co.uk
Tottenham Court Road

COFFEE PRICING.

Espresso	£1.50 / £1.80
Cappuccino	£2.40
Latte	£2.40
Flat white	£2.40

OPEN.

Mon-Fri.	8:00am - 7:00pm
Sat.	9:00am - 6:00pm
Sun.	Closed

OVERVIEW.

Category
Artisanal Independent
Owner
Richard Lilley
Head barista
Matthew Malby
First opened
2010

COFFEE & EQUIPMENT.

Coffee roaster
Has Bean, Square Mile and others
Coffee machine
La Marzocco Strada EP, 3 groups
Coffee grinder
Mazzer Robur E, Mazzer Super Jolly, Anfim Super Caimano

Sister coffee shops.
Tottenham Court Road

Tapped & Packed specialises in **brewed coffee (filter, cafetiere and AeroPress)**

Tapped & Packed Tottenham Crt Rd

114 Tottenham Court Road, W1T 5AH

This second Tapped & Packed location boasts the same impeccable coffee credentials as its sister venue and the unique, glass-backed, customised Nuova Simonelli Aurelia was moved here from the Rathbone Place store. Different types of beans are used for milk coffees and espressos at Tapped & Packed, and yet another coffee menu is available for filter options at the brew bar. The interior features a tree-stump podium in the centre, washed steel, exposed light bulbs and white ceramic that recall London's Victorian heyday while offering a welcoming space to enjoy cake or a leisurely lunch.

FOOD.

Fresh sandwiches and savouries, delicious cakes and soups in a copper tureen.

CONTACT.

+44(0)20 7580 2163
www.tappedandpacked.co.uk
postmaster@tappedandpacked.co.uk
Warren Street

OPEN.

Mon-Fri.	8:00am - 7:00pm
Sat.	10:00am - 6:00pm
Sun.	Closed

OVERVIEW.

Category
Artisanal Independent
Owner
Richard Lilley
Head barista
Sang Ho Park
First opened
June 2011

COFFEE & EQUIPMENT.

Coffee roaster
Has Bean, Square Mile and others
Coffee machine
Nuova Simonelli Aurelia, 3 groups, customised
Coffee grinder
Mazzer x 3

COFFEE PRICING.

Espresso	£1.50 / £1.80
Cappuccino	£2.40
Latte	£2.40
Flat white	£2.40

Sister coffee shops.
Rathbone Place

RATING.

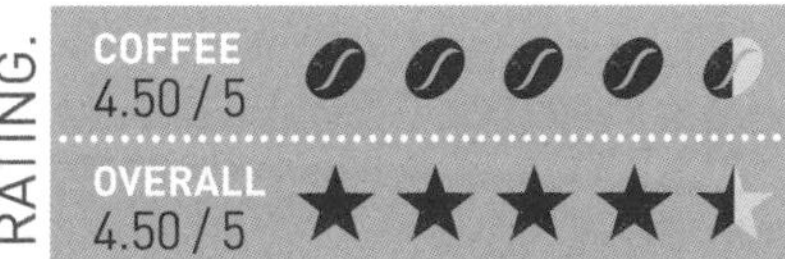

Soho

Famous for its outrageous nightlife, Soho is also well-known for its cutting-edge bars, clubs and restaurants. This spirit of experimentation and adventure extends to coffee and many of London's most exciting artisanal cafés can be found here.

Bar Italia

22 Frith Street, W1D 4RP

One of London's oldest and most famous coffee shops, Bar Italia has been a Soho institution since 1949. Now owned and run by the grandchildren of original owners Lou and Caterina Polledri, the walls of the bar are covered with framed photographs of the stars of sports and showbiz who have frequented the venue over the years. The unofficial home of Italians in London, this is the place to be when Italy is playing anyone at football, and the best café to get genuine Italian-style espresso prepared the old-fashioned way.

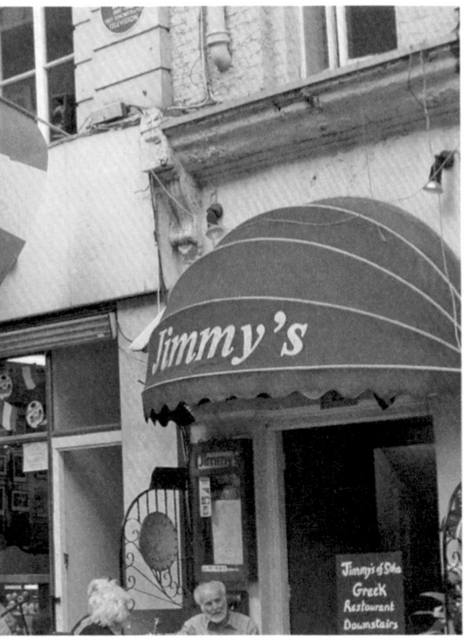

OPEN.

Mon-Sun. Open 24 hours

OVERVIEW.

Category
Eatery
Owner
Antonio Polledri
First opened
1949

COFFEE & EQUIPMENT.

Coffee roaster
Signor Angelucci
Coffee machine
Gaggia, 4 groups
Coffee grinder
Mazzer

COFFEE PRICING.

Espresso	£2.20 / £3.20
Cappuccino	£2.90 / £3.40
Latte	£3.00 / £3.70

FOOD.

Traditional Italian fare.

CONTACT.

+44(0)20 7437 4520
www.baritaliasoho.co.uk
info@baritaliasoho.co.uk
Leicester Square

RATING.

COFFEE 4.25 / 5

OVERALL 4.25 / 5

Fernandez & Wells Beak Street

73 Beak Street, W1F 9SR

This venue perfected Fernandez & Wells' signature combination of artisanal European food with superb coffee and remains one of London's premier foodie destinations. Now with sister venues that include an espresso bar, wine bar and eatery, this café retains its simple focus on good coffee and food, complemented by cream walls and rustic timber benches that encourage visitors to appreciate the quality of the produce on offer.

Sister coffee shops.
St Anne's Court / Lexington Street / Somerset House

OPEN.

Mon-Fri. 7:30am - 6:00pm
Sat. 9:00am - 6:00pm
Sun. 10:00am - 5:00pm

OVERVIEW.

Category
Artisanal Independent
Owner
Jorge Fernandez and Rick Wells
Head barista
Alex Mackinnon
First opened
2007

COFFEE & EQUIPMENT.

Coffee roaster
Has Bean Coffee
Coffee machine
Synesso Cyncra, 3 groups
Coffee grinder
Mazzer Robur, Mazzer Robur E, Ditting

COFFEE PRICING.

Espresso £2.30
Cappuccino £2.60
Latte £2.60
Flat white £2.60

FOOD.

An alluring spread of sandwiches, baguettes and deli-style foods are beautifully presented on stone benches.

CONTACT.

+44(0)20 7287 8124
www.fernandezandwells.com
taste@fernandezandwells.com
Piccadilly Circus

RATING.

COFFEE 4.50 / 5

OVERALL 4.50 / 5

Flat White

17 Berwick Street, W1F 0PT

Flat White has been firmly established as a London insitution since opening in 2005 with the aim of introducing Antipodean-style coffee to London. A mecca for Kiwis and Aussies longing for a touch of home or anyone looking for a superb coffee experience, Flat White has kept in touch with its grungy and unpretentious roots without sacrificing its edge. Staff are well up to date with the newest developments in coffee brewing methods such as cold filters, and the vast, custom-built 4-group Synesso Hydra (dubbed "The Orca") is kept humming all day by crowds of Soho regulars.

OPEN.

Mon-Fri. 8:00am - 7:00pm
Sat-Sun. 9:00am - 6:00pm

OVERVIEW.

Category
Artisanal Independent
Owner
Cameron McClure and Peter Hall
First opened
2005

COFFEE & EQUIPMENT.

Coffee roaster
Square Mile Coffee Roasters
Coffee machine
Custom-built Synesso Hydra, 4 groups
Coffee grinder
Mazzer Robur E, Mazzer Decaf, Anfim

Sister coffee shops.
Milkbar

COFFEE PRICING.

Espresso	£2.00 / £2.20
Cappuccino	£3.00
Latte	£3.00
Flat white	£2.50

FOOD.

Made-to-order salads, chunky sandwiches, all-day breakfast and brunch menu.

CONTACT.

+44(0)20 7734 0370
www.flatwhitecafe.com
flattie@flat-white.co.uk
Oxford Circus

Single-estate espresso and **cold-drip coffees** are also available

RATING.

COFFEE 4.75 / 5

OVERALL 4.25 / 5

Foxcroft & Ginger

3 Berwick Street, W1F 0DR

OPEN.

Mon.	7:30am - 5:00pm
Tue-Fri.	8:00am - 9:00pm
Sat.	9:00am - 9:00pm
Sun.	9:00am - 7:00pm

This stylish Soho coffee house has quickly become a key part of the vibrant Berwick Street community. A heavy wooden door leads into an industrial space decorated with a mixture of concrete, tile, brick and exposed piping, and the downstairs area offers a welcome retreat. Climpson's espresso is made using a shiny Synesso Cyncra and perfectly complements the range of locally sourced food on offer that includes gourmet sandwiches.

FOOD.

Fresh salads, croissants, baguettes and cakes are made on site from locally sourced produce.

CONTACT.

+44(0)20 7287 5890
www.foxcroftandginger.co.uk
info@foxcroftandginger.co.uk
Oxford Circus

OVERVIEW.

Category
Artisanal Independent
Owner
Quintin Dawson
Head barista
Joe Collins
First opened
2010

COFFEE & EQUIPMENT.

Coffee roaster
Climpson & Sons
Coffee machine
Synesso Cyncra, 3 groups
Coffee grinder
Anfim

COFFEE PRICING.

Espresso	£2.00
Cappuccino	£2.40
Latte	£2.40
Flat white	£2.40

RATING.

COFFEE 4.00 / 5

OVERALL 4.00 / 5

TOP 30

Milkbar

3 Bateman Street, W1D 4AG

OPEN.

Mon-Fri.	8:00am - 7:00pm
Sat-Sun.	9:00am - 6:00pm

 decaf   

Milkbar has emerged from beneath the wing of Flat White to become one of Soho's most popular venues, serving consistently excellent coffee to the creative crowd of Soho. The café's youthful, grungy feel and rotating art exhibitions make this a favourite hangout, as does the all-day breakfast and brunch menu, which includes milkshakes.

FOOD.

All-day breakfast and brunch, fresh salads, sandwiches and sweet snacks.

CONTACT.

+44(0)20 7287 4796
flattie@flat-white.co.uk
Leicester Square

Sister coffee shops.
Flat White

OVERVIEW.

Category
Artisanal Independent
Owner
Cameron McClure
First opened
2008

COFFEE & EQUIPMENT.

Coffee roaster
Square Mile Coffee Roasters
Coffee machine
La Marzocco FB/80, 3 groups
Coffee grinder
Anfim, Mazzer x 2, Ditting

COFFEE PRICING.

Espresso	£2.00
Cappuccino	£2.50 / £3.00
Latte	£2.50 / £3.00
Flat white	£2.50

RATING.

COFFEE 4.50 / 5

OVERALL 4.25 / 5

Nordic Bakery

14a Golden Square, W1F 9JG

The trend for all things Scandinavian finds its perfect expression in this authentic Finnish bakery and café. Cinnamon buns, rye bread snacks and spiced biscuits are served in a dim, serene space where candles flicker on tables and customers chat in hushed tones. Music is absent and wifi is deliberately not on offer, allowing customers to truly switch off and enjoy a relaxing coffee and freshly baked Nordic treat.

Sister coffee shops.
Marylebone

OPEN.

Mon-Fri. 8:00am - 8:00pm
Sat. 9:00am - 7:00pm
Sun. 11:00am - 6:00pm

OVERVIEW.

Category
Bakery Coffee Shop
Owner
Jali Wahlsten and Miisa Mink
First opened
2007

COFFEE & EQUIPMENT.

Coffee roaster
Dibar
Coffee machine
Wega, 2 groups
Coffee grinder
Mazzer, Ditting

COFFEE PRICING.

Espresso £1.60
Cappuccino £2.20
Latte £2.40

FOOD.

Scandinavian sweets and savouries baked freshly on site each day.

CONTACT.

+44(0)20 3230 1077
www.nordicbakery.com
info@nordicbakery.com
Piccadilly Circus

RATING.

COFFEE 3.75 / 5

OVERALL 4.00 / 5

Nude Espresso Soho Square

19 Soho Square, W1D 3QN

Nude Espresso's signature East blend coffee has arrived in Soho. The interior here is sleeker and more understated than Nude Hanbury Street, but the staff are just as passionate about delivering excellent coffee to their urbane Soho customers. The Toper roaster in the front window speaks volumes about this venue's dedication to good coffee and Nude beans are available to buy in large 1kg bags. A range of tasty breakfast, lunch and sweet foods are served with a smile along with a coffee menu that includes pourover and AeroPress options.

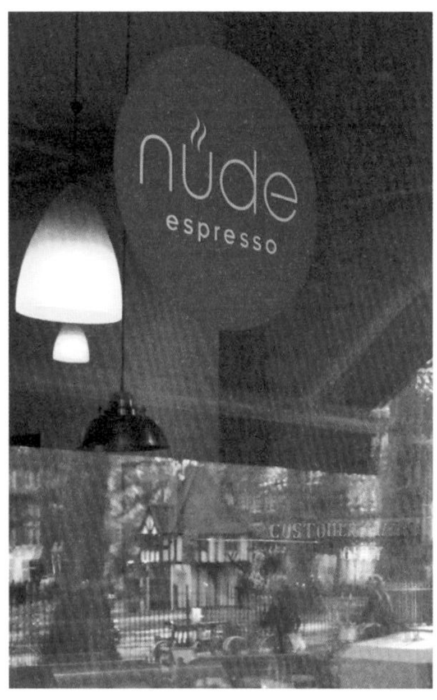

OPEN.

Mon-Fri. 8:00am - 5:00pm
Sat-Sun. 11:00am - 6:00pm

OVERVIEW.

Category
Artisanal Independent
Owner
Richard Reed
Head barista
Kurtis Leigh
First opened
May 2011

COFFEE & EQUIPMENT.

Coffee roaster
Nude Espresso
Coffee machine
Wega Nova, 2 groups
Coffee grinder
Wega

Sister coffee shops.
Hanbury Street /
Brick Lane (Roastery)

COFFEE PRICING.

Espresso	£2.00
Cappuccino	£2.50
Latte	£2.50
Flat white	£2.50

FOOD.

Croissants, brownies, cakes and cookies baked daily at Nude Hanbury Street, and a savoury breakfast and lunch menu.

Nude Espresso roasts its own coffee at a roastery on Brick Lane (Old Truman Brewery)

CONTACT.

+44(0)77 3873 4019
www.nudeespresso.com
rich@nudeespresso.com
Tottenham Court Rd

RATING.

Princi

135 Wardour Street, W1F 0UT

OPEN.

Mon-Sat. 7:00am - 12:00am
Sun. 8:30am - 10:00pm

Sleek, stylish Princi is the first London outlet of an established Italian bakery chain, brought to this city by Alan Yau of Wagamama fame. A buzzing, lively eatery, Princi is a perfect fit for Soho and is jam-packed with hungry customers all hours of the day and night. One length of the venue is occupied by tantalising displays of croissants, tarts, cakes, pizza and salads all freshly made on site. The elegant dining area consists of granite tables and a long metal bench against a water-feature wall, and the large window frontage is perfect for people-watching on this entertaining street.

FOOD.

Pizzas baked in the stone oven, an endless array of pastries, plus a selection of salads and hot meals.

CONTACT.

+44(0)20 7478 8888
www.princi.co.uk
email@princi.co.uk
Tottenham Court Rd

OVERVIEW.

Category
Eatery
Owner
Rocco Princi and Alan Yau
Head barista
Vincent WIlliams
First opened
2008

COFFEE & EQUIPMENT.

Coffee roaster
Monmouth Coffee Company
Coffee machine
La Marzocco Linea, 3 groups
Coffee grinder
Mazzer Luigi

COFFEE PRICING.

Espresso	£1.60
Cappuccino	£2.30
Latte	£2.30
Flat white	£2.40

Sister coffee shops.
Four Princi bakeries in Milan

RATING.

COFFEE 4.00 / 5

OVERALL 4.25 / 5

Sacred Ganton Street

TOP 30

13 Ganton Street, W1F 9BL

Image supplied by Sacred

OPEN.

Mon-Fri. 7:30am - 8:00pm
Sat-Sun. 10:00am - 7:00pm

The Sacred empire now extends across six London locations but this is where it all began back in 2005. Owners Tubbs Wanigasekera and Matt Clark are proud New Zealanders and this shines through in the decor and relaxed atmosphere that characterises this busy café. While the main upstairs area has a pleasing openness that extends out into the bustle of Carnaby Street, couches in the mellow basement offer a cosy refuge in which to sip a cup of the delicious New Zealand-style house roast.

FOOD.

All-day menu of breakfast, bagels, sandwiches, cakes and pastries.

CONTACT.

+44(0)20 7734 1415
www.sacredcafe.co.uk
globalcoffee@gmail.com
Oxford Circus

Sister coffee shops.
Covent Garden / Highbury Studios / Westfield / Kingly Court / Torrington Street

OVERVIEW.

Category
Chain
Owner
Tubbs Wanigasekera and Matt Clark
Head barista
Liz Douglas
First opened
2005

COFFEE & EQUIPMENT.

Coffee roaster
Sacred house roast
Coffee machine
La Marzocco Linea, 2 groups
Coffee grinder
Anfim Super Caimano, Mazzer Super Jolly

COFFEE PRICING.

Espresso	£1.60
Cappuccino	£2.50 / £2.70
Latte	£2.50 / £2.70
Flat white	£2.50 / £2.70

RATING.

COFFEE 4.25 / 5

OVERALL 4.25 / 5

Speakeasy

3 Lowndes Court, W1F 7HD

This new venture from the The Coffeesmiths Collective brings a much-needed injection of authenticity to the slick shopping district of Carnaby Street. Lovingly prepared Climpson's coffee and locally supplied food is served in a light, white space, but this is only half the story - downstairs houses an ambient brew bar, where weary shoppers can be revived by the fragrant flavours of single-origin filter coffees. Pour your own or ask a staff member to talk you through this true coffee experience and be transported to the hills of countries such as Argentina or El Salvador via the zesty flavours of Speakeasy's ever-changing menu.

OPEN.

Mon-Wed.	8:00am - 7:00pm
Thu-Fri.	8:00am - 8:00pm
Sat.	11:00am - 8:00pm
Sun.	11:00am - 6:00pm

OVERVIEW.

Category
Artisanal Independent
Owner
Tim Ridley and Chris McKie
Head barista
Mel Tuoma
First opened
September 2011

COFFEE & EQUIPMENT.

Coffee roaster
Climpson & Sons
Coffee machine
La Marzocco, 3 groups
Coffee grinder
Mazzer

Sister coffee shops.
Department of Coffee
& Social Affairs

COFFEE PRICING.

Espresso	£2.00
Cappuccino	£2.60 / £2.90
Latte	£2.60 / £2.90
Flat white	£2.60 / £2.90

FOOD.

The standard range of cakes, pastries and sandwiches are both locally supplied and made in-house.

CONTACT.

www.speakeasycoffee.co.uk
Oxford Circus

RATING.
COFFEE 4.50 / 5
OVERALL 4.50 / 5

Starbucks Conduit Street

2-3 Conduit Street, W1S 2BX

Image supplied by Starbucks

OPEN.

Mon-Wed.	6:30am - 9:00pm
Thu-Fri.	6:30am - 10:00pm
Sat.	7:30am - 10:00pm
Sun.	8:00am - 9:00pm

This Conduit Street concept store scales back the usual Starbucks branding in favour of a more subtle approach. Wooden, earthy tones replace the standard dark green colour scheme and help to create a more relaxing environment. The basement is an open space with a lounge feel that includes private areas for business meetings or catch-ups with friends.

FOOD.

Signature Starbucks sandwiches, paninis, muffins and cakes.

CONTACT.

+44(0)20 7493 9754
www.starbucks.co.uk
ukinfo@starbucks.com
Oxford Circus

Sister coffee shops.
Approximately 300 stores in London

Pourover filter coffees and **special-reserve espressos** are also available

OVERVIEW.

Category
Chain
Owner
Starbucks Corporation
First opened
2009

COFFEE & EQUIPMENT.

Coffee roaster
Starbucks Roast
Coffee machine
Mastrena
Coffee grinder
Ditting

COFFEE PRICING.

Espresso	£1.45 / £1.75
Cappuccino	£2.15 / £2.50 / £2.75
Latte	£2.15 / £2.50 / £2.75
Flat white	£2.40

RATING.

COFFEE 3.75 / 5

OVERALL 4.25 / 5

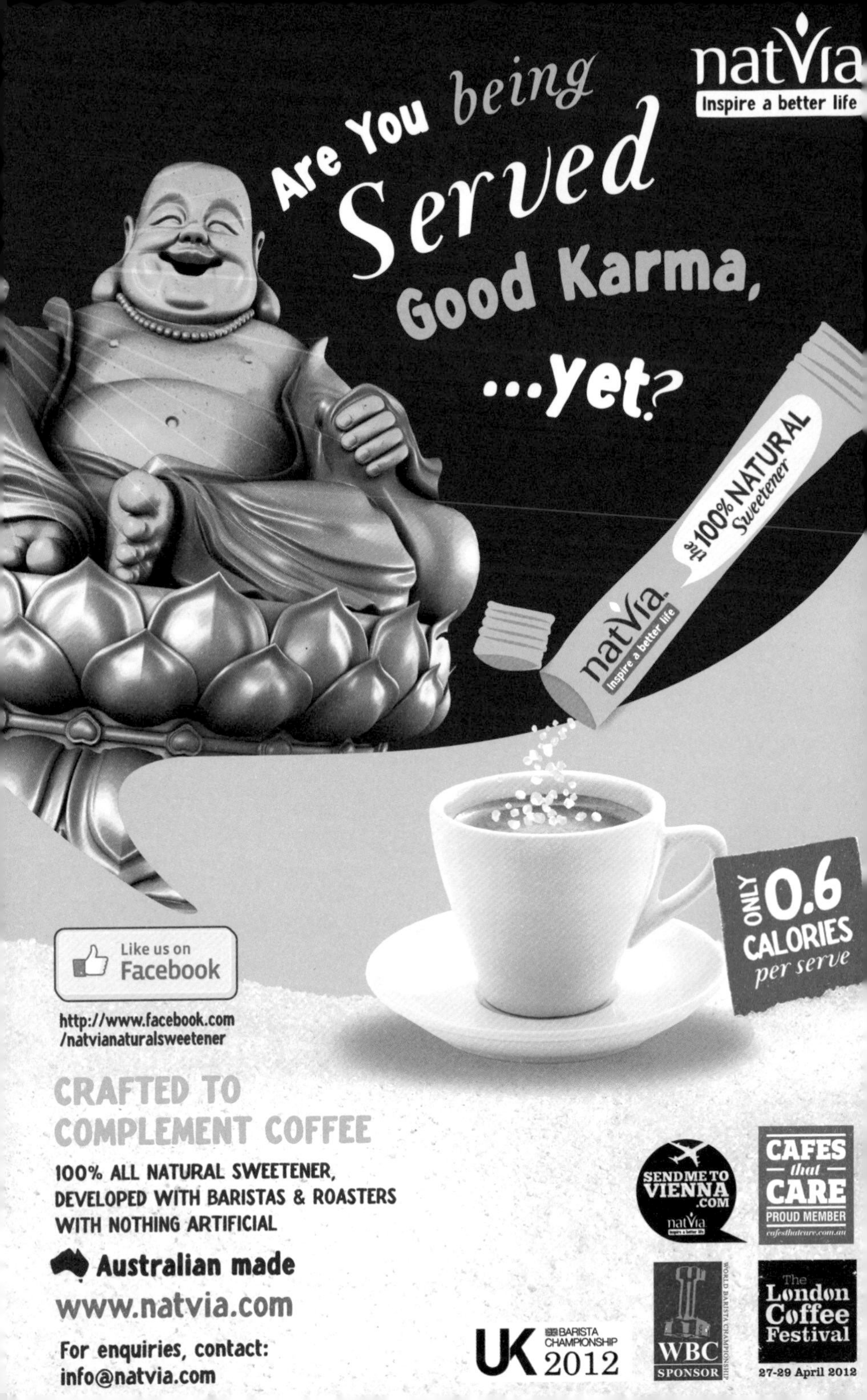
natvia
Inspire a better life
Are You being Served Good Karma, ...yet?
the 100% NATURAL Sweetener
natvia
Inspire a better life
ONLY 0.6 CALORIES per serve
Like us on Facebook
http://www.facebook.com
/natvianaturalsweetener
CRAFTED TO COMPLEMENT COFFEE
100% ALL NATURAL SWEETENER,
DEVELOPED WITH BARISTAS & ROASTERS
WITH NOTHING ARTIFICIAL
Australian made
www.natvia.com
For enquiries, contact:
info@natvia.com
SEND ME TO VIENNA.COM
CAFES that CARE
PROUD MEMBER
cafesthatcare.com.au
UK BARISTA CHAMPIONSHIP 2012
WBC SPONSOR
WORLD BARISTA CHAMPIONSHIP
The London Coffee Festival
27-29 April 2012

Farringdon & Clerkenwell

Formerly hubs of manufacturing and enterprise, the districts of Farringdon and Clerkenwell now house smart offices, loft apartments, night clubs and restaurants. Many of the most exciting new coffee venues in town can also be found here, making this the new heart of London's burgeoning coffee culture.

TOP 30

Caravan

11-13 Exmouth Market, EC1R 4QD

Image supplied by Caravan

OPEN.

Mon-Fri.	8:00am - 12:00am
Sat.	10:00am - 12:00am
Sun.	10:00am - 4:00pm

Since opening in 2010, Caravan roastery and restaurant has rapidly become a popular fixture on the diverse Exmouth Market food and coffee scene. Its modern dining space is always busy, particularly on sunny days when patrons spill out onto the pavement. Plenty of options on the menu make this a popular destination for a weekend brunch or casual dinner. As well as espresso, a wide variety of coffee brewing methods are on offer, allowing patrons to appreciate the full range of flavours found in Caravan house roasts.

FOOD.

An all-day fusion food menu offers plenty of delicious choices.

CONTACT.

+44(0)20 7833 8115
www.caravanonexmouth.co.uk
coffee@caravanonexmouth.co.uk
Farringdon

Single-origin filter coffees are available via **pourover, AeroPress,** and various other brewing methods

OVERVIEW.

Category
Eatery
Owner
Chris Ammermann, Jedediah Coleman and Miles Kirby
First opened
2010

COFFEE & EQUIPMENT.

Coffee roaster
Caravan
Coffee machine
La Marzocco Linea, 3 groups
Coffee grinder
Anfim, Mazzer Robur E, Ditting

COFFEE PRICING.

Espresso	£1.80 / £2.00
Cappuccino	£2.60
Latte	£2.60
Flat white	£2.60

RATING.

COFFEE 4.50 / 5

OVERALL 4.50 / 5

Coco di Mama

90 Fleet Street, EC4Y 1DH

OPEN.

Mon-Fri. 6:30am - 5:00pm
Sat-Sun. Closed

Coco di Mama's goal is to bring quick, high-quality Italian food and coffee to busy Londoners, and offers something new to those who prefer a slicker coffee experience.
This new concept has proved extremely popular since it opened in April 2011 and childhood friends Daniel Land and Jeremy Sanders have big plans for their fledgling business. The Climpsons coffee served here is strong and hot - just the way the bankers like it - and comes with a chocolate on the side, for a sweet touch.

FOOD.

Quick-service pasta, along with a wide range of baguettes, salads, soups, snacks and treats.

CONTACT.

+44(0)20 7583 9277
cocodimama.co.uk
daniel@cocodimama.co.uk
St. Paul's

OVERVIEW.

Category
Eatery
Owner
Daniel Land and Jeremy Sanders
Head barista
Matthew Randell
First opened
April 2011

COFFEE & EQUIPMENT.

Coffee roaster
Climpson & Sons
Coffee machine
La Marzocco Linea, 3 groups
Coffee grinder
Mazzer Robur E

COFFEE PRICING.

Espresso	£1.40 / £1.60
Cappuccino	£2.00 / £2.20
Latte	£2.00 / £2.20
Flat white	£2.00

RATING.

COFFEE
4.25 / 5

OVERALL
4.00 / 5

Department of Coffee & Social Affairs

14-16 Leather Lane , EC1N 7SU

OPEN.

Mon-Fri. 7:00am - 6:00pm
Sat-Sun. 10:00am - 4:00pm

The boldly named Department of Coffee and Social Affairs is a key player on the booming Farringdon coffee scene. Occupying a former ironmonger's premises across two shopfronts on Leather Lane, this generous space features an unpolished wood and exposed brick theme and plentiful seating. The Department offers an alternative to the Square Mile coffee served by most in the vicinity, with its regular espresso provided by Climpson & Sons alongside alternating guest blends. Owners the Coffeesmiths Collective also run coffee making and tasting classes after hours.

FOOD.

Fresh baguettes, sandwiches, quiche, cakes and brownies.

CONTACT.

www.departmentofcoffee.co.uk
shop@departmentofcoffee.co.uk
Farringdon

Sister coffee shops.
Speakeasy

OVERVIEW.

Category
Artisanal Independent
Owner
Tim Ridley and Chris McKie
Head barista
Chris McKie
First opened
2010

COFFEE & EQUIPMENT.

Coffee roaster
Climpson & Sons
Coffee machine
La Marzocco FB/80, 3 groups
Coffee grinder
Mazzer Robur E x 2, Mazzer Super Jolly

COFFEE PRICING.

Espresso	£2.00
Cappuccino	£2.50 / £2.80
Latte	£2.50 / £2.80
Flat white	£2.30

RATING.

TOP 30

Dose Espresso

69 Long Lane, EC1A 9EJ

Dose Espresso is widely recognised as a leader in London's artisanal coffee scene. Owner and barista James Phillips sets the standard in his small but welcoming espresso bar, using a Square Mile seasonal roast and featuring a weekly guest espresso blend. All Dose coffee, milk and ingredients are ethically sourced and environmental consciousness is an important part of the café's identity. Dose's new premises feature a striking red, black and white colour scheme, and coffee-making and tasting classes are now also offered.

FOOD.

Small breakfast menu, freshly prepared salads and sandwiches, and an assortment of sweet treats.

CONTACT.

+44(0)20 7600 0382
www.dose-espresso.com
james@dose-espresso.com
Barbican

OPEN.

Mon-Fri.	7:00am - 5:00pm
Sat.	9:00am - 4:00pm
Sun.	Closed

OVERVIEW.

Category
Artisanal Independent
Owner / Head barista
James Phillips
First opened
2009

COFFEE & EQUIPMENT.

Coffee roaster
Square Mile Coffee Roasters and guest espresso from various roasters
Coffee machine
La Marzocco FB/80, 3 groups
Coffee grinder
Anfim Super Caimano, Anfim Best and Mahlkönig Vario

COFFEE PRICING.

Espresso	£1.70 / £2.00
Cappuccino	£2.50 / £3.00
Latte	£2.40 / £2.90
Flat white	£2.50 / £3.00

RATING.

COFFEE 4.50 / 5

OVERALL 4.25 / 5

Farm Collective

91 Cowcross Street, EC1M 6BH

OPEN.

Mon-Fri. 7:00am-3:30pm
Sat-Sun. Closed

Farm Collective takes pride in sourcing high-quality, fresh, ethical produce directly from British farms. This emphasis on quality extends to the coffee - excellent Square Mile espresso is pulled through a Synesso Cyncra and can be enjoyed along with a signature peanut butter brownie. The tantalising food display makes this a great destination for a quick drop-in or more substantial options are available if a lazy lunch is more your speed.

FOOD.

"Fresh food prepared daily" - breakfast, gourmet sandwiches, pies and various daily specials.

CONTACT.

+44(0)20 7253 2142
www.farmcollective.com
craig@farmcollective.com
Farringdon

OVERVIEW.

Category
Artisanal Independent
Owner
Dominic Kamara and Craig Wills
First opened
2009

COFFEE & EQUIPMENT.

Coffee roaster
Square Mile Coffee Roasters
Coffee machine
Synesso Cyncra, 2 groups
Coffee grinder
Anfim

COFFEE PRICING.

Espresso	£1.70 / £2.10
Cappuccino	£2.10 / £2.40
Latte	£2.10 / £2.40
Flat white	£2.20 / £2.50

RATING.

COFFEE 4.00 / 5

OVERALL 3.75 / 5

Get Coffee

3 Fleet Street, EC4Y 1AU

OPEN.

Mon-Fri.	6:30am - 7:00pm
Sat.	8:00am - 5:30pm
Sun.	Closed

Combining the accessibility of a coffee chain store with the personal touch of an independent, Get Coffee is a unique and appealing coffee destination in the heart of the City of London. Occupying a heritage-listed building on Fleet Street, Get Coffee serves Butterworth & Son espresso, freshly ground American-style filter coffee and a wide selection of house-blend loose leaf teas to a mixed crowd of lawyers, bankers, students and tourists. A variety of lunch options are also available to take away or eat in the modern downstairs area.

FOOD.

Fresh baguettes, paninis, soups and a selection of cakes, slices and flavoured macarons from a local bakery and patisserie.

CONTACT.

+44(0)20 7583 7757
andy@getcoffee.org.uk
Temple

OVERVIEW.

Category
Artisanal Independent
Owner
Andy Wells
Head barista
Nerijus Latakas
First opened
January 2011

COFFEE & EQUIPMENT.

Coffee roaster
Butterworth & Son
Coffee machine
Brasilia Opus Tall, 3 groups
Coffee grinder
Mazzer Super Jolly

COFFEE PRICING.

Espresso	£1.45 / £1.75
Cappuccino	£2.15 / £2.45 / £2.75
Latte	£2.15 / £2.45 / £2.75
Flat white	£2.35

RATING.

COFFEE
4.00 / 5

OVERALL
3.75 / 5

Prufrock Coffee Leather Lane

23-25 Leather Lane, EC1N 7TE

London coffee geeks now have a spiritual home in the form of Gwilym Davies and Jeremy Challender's Prufrock Coffee on Leather Lane. This impressive venue boasts not only a Nuova Simonelli and a Kees van der Westen, but also a full brew bar featuring every brewing method you've heard of (and probably a few more). The light, open space follows the minimal, industrial template that many coffee shops are adopting, but adds something extra in details such as vintage coffee ephemera, bottles of Vichy Catalan water and bespoke coffee cups stamped with pictures of cute animals.

Extremely knowledgeable staff are on hand to brew superb coffee served with 4, 6 or 8oz of milk - these measurements replace conventional titles such as latte or flat white - and host coffee classes, tastings and workshops downstairs.

SOYA

OPEN.

Mon-Fri.	8:00am - 6:00pm
Sat.	10:00am - 4:30pm
Sun.	11:00am - 4:30pm

OVERVIEW.

Category
Artisanal Independent
Owner
Gwilym Davies and Jeremy Challender
First opened
February 2011

COFFEE & EQUIPMENT.

Coffee roaster
Square Mile Coffee Roasters
Coffee machine
Nuova Simonelli, Kees van der Westen Spirit and others
Coffee grinder
Mazzer Robur, Mahlkönig Tanzania, Nuova Simonelli Mythos and various others

COFFEE PRICING.

Espresso	£1.80
Cappuccino	£2.20 / £2.40
Latte	£2.60
Flat white	£2.20

FOOD.

A tempting selection of tarts, croissants and cakes, breakfast porridge, and a compact gourmet lunch menu.

CONTACT.

+44(0)7853 483479
www.prufrockcoffee.com
info@prufrockcoffee.com
Farringdon

The extensive **brew bar** offers a range of coffees made using methods including **syphon, AeroPress, pourover** and **cold drip**

RATING.

COFFEE 4.75 / 5

OVERALL 4.75 / 5

St. Ali

27 Clerkenwell Road, EC1M 5RN

This Australian-owned café, restaurant and roastery has proved to be a game-changer since arriving in London in 2011. Spanning multiple floors decorated in natural wood and chic stainless steel, this Clerkenwell venue features a downstairs coffee bar offering a range of expertly prepared coffees, a gleaming 12kg roaster and an upstairs dining area that is regularly packed to the rafters with hungry brunch customers. Australian and Pacific influences blend with local ingredients and a unique coffee roast to make this a truly cutting-edge venue that provides a vision of what London's coffee scene could look like in the near future.

OPEN.

Daily: 7:00am - 6:00pm

OVERVIEW.

Category
Eatery
Owner
Long Black Limited
Head barista
Baptiste Kreyder
First opened
April 2011

COFFEE & EQUIPMENT.

Coffee roaster
St. Ali
Coffee machine
Synesso Cyncra, 3 groups and La Marzocco Linea, 2 groups
Coffee grinder
Mazzer Luigi srl and Mazzer Robur E

CONTACT.

+44(0)20 7253 5754
www.stali.co.uk
info@stali.co.uk
Farringdon

Coffee is roasted on site.
Also offer **pourover, brewed coffee** and AeroPress

COFFEE PRICING.

Espresso	£2.00
Cappuccino	£2.40
Latte	£2.60
Flat white	£2.40

FOOD.

Modern Australian-inspired menu with delicious breakfast and lunch options including corn fritters, organic eggs, salads and tarts.

Sister coffee shops.
Sensory Lab

RATING.

COFFEE 4.75 / 5
OVERALL 4.75 / 5

Camden & Islington

Stretching from the banks of the Thames to the leafy streets of Hampstead, the districts of Camden and Islington contain a huge variety of cafés and restaurants, from the stylish venues of the central city to the colourful market stalls of Camden and chic North London delis.

Bea's of Bloomsbury

44 Theobald's Road, WC1X 8NW

OPEN.

Mon-Fri. 8:00am - 7:00pm
Sat-Sun. 12:00am - 7:00pm

The selection of baked goods and treats on display at Bea's is enough to make any cake-lover go weak at the knees. Customers can purchase a selection of cakes to go, or enjoy lunch or afternoon tea while watching the bakery's famous treats being created in the kitchen at the rear of the café. Fresh Square Mile coffee provides the perfect accompaniment for a decadent chocolate cupcake or even a slice of espresso bourbon cake for a double caffeine hit.

FOOD.

A wide range of cakes and sweets, plus a full lunch menu.

CONTACT.

+44(0)20 7242 8330
www.beasofbloomsbury.com
contact@beasofbloomsbury.com
⊖ Chancery Lane

Sister coffee shops.
One New Change, St. Paul's / King's Road / Maltby Street Market

OVERVIEW.

Category
Bakery Coffee Shop
Owner
Bea Vo
Head barista
Kristina Johansson
First opened
2008

COFFEE & EQUIPMENT.

Coffee roaster
Square Mile Coffee Roasters
Coffee machine
La Marzocco Linea, 2 groups
Coffee grinder
Anfim, Mazzer

COFFEE PRICING.

Espresso	£1.70 / £2.00
Cappuccino	£2.40 / £2.70
Latte	£2.40 / £2.70
Flat white	£2.40 / £2.70

RATING.

COFFEE 4.00 / 5

OVERALL 4.00 / 5

Coffee Circus Crouch End

136 Crouch Hill, N8 9DX

OPEN.

Mon-Fri.	8:00am - 7:00pm
Sat-Sun.	8.30am - 7:00pm

Located in Crouch Hill, where good coffee is hard to find, Coffee Circus is a great reason to make the journey north. With its vintage tearoom feel and circus theme, this café offers a warm and friendly space in which to meet for coffee and cake, but its links to the Coffee Circus tuk tuk and kiosk at Camden Market also give it urban London caché. Delicious cakes and savouries are sold alongside a wide range of teas and coffee beans from various London roasteries.

FOOD.

A breakfast and brunch menu, sandwiches, soups and homemade cakes - all organic and Fairtrade where possible.

CONTACT.

+44(0)75 0755 1472
www.coffeecircus.co.uk
Crouch Hill

Sister coffee shops.
Camden Lock / Camden Stables

OVERVIEW.

Category
Artisanal Independent
Owner
Gedas Siminavicius
Head barista
Roland Mackevicius
First opened
January 2011

COFFEE & EQUIPMENT.

Coffee roaster
Climpson & Sons house blend
Coffee machine
La Marzocco FB/90, 2 groups
Coffee grinder
Anfim, Vario, Ditting

COFFEE PRICING.

Espresso	£1.80
Cappuccino	£2.50
Latte	£2.50
Flat white	£2.50

RATING.

COFFEE 3.75 / 5

OVERALL 3.75 / 5

The Espresso Room

31-35 Great Ormond Street, WC1N 3HZ

The Espresso Room is a simple concept: take a tiny space, add a Synesso espresso machine, Mazzer grinder, Square Mile coffee and an owner who is passionate and knowledgeable, and the result is consistently excellent coffee. Space may be limited but the chic wooden decor is warm and stylish, and this espresso bar is widely considered one of London's best coffee venues. Join the queue of hospital staff, lawyers, Lamb's Conduit fashionistas and local residents and discover why.

TOP 30

COFFEE PRICING.

Espresso	£1.60 / £2.00
Cappuccino	£2.60 / £3.10
Latte	£2.60 / £3.10
Flat white	£2.60 / £3.10

FOOD.

A small selection of cakes, pastries and freshly made sandwiches.

CONTACT.

+44(0)77 6071 4883
www.theespressoroom.com
info@theespressoroom.com
Russell Square

OPEN.

Mon-Fri. 7:30am - 5:00pm
Sat-Sun. Closed
(Open Saturdays during summer)

OVERVIEW.

Category
Artisanal Independent
Owner
Ben Townsend
First opened
2009

COFFEE & EQUIPMENT.

Coffee roaster
Square Mile Coffee Roasters, Has Bean
Coffee machine
Synesso Cyncra, 2 groups
Coffee grinder
Mazzer Robur E, Vario

RATING.

COFFEE 4.50 / 5

OVERALL 4.25 / 5

Fix

161 Whitecross Street, EC1Y 8JL

OPEN.

Mon-Fri. 7:00am - 7:00pm
Sat-Sun. 8:00am - 7:00pm

Discreetly occupying a former pub on Whitecross Street, Fix is a spacious and stylish place to drop in for a coffee and bite to eat. Big leather couches, well-chosen vintage furniture and quirky light fittings make this a comfortable and dynamic space in which to hang out and use the free wifi. Creatives and visitors to the weekday Whitecross Street Market keep Fix buzzing and make it a favourite destination for coffee lovers.

FOOD.

Takeaway sandwiches and salads, hearty soups and tempting bakery

CONTACT.

+44(0)20 7998 3878
www.fix-coffee.co.uk
sashafixcoffee@gmail.com
Old Street

Sister coffee shops.
Fix 126

OVERVIEW.

Category
Artisanal Independent
Owner
Sasha Rainey
First opened
2009

COFFEE & EQUIPMENT.

Coffee roaster
Climpson & Sons seasonal blend
Coffee machine
La Marzocco Linea PID, 3 groups
Coffee grinder
Mazzer Robur E, Mazzer Super Jolly E

COFFEE PRICING.

Espresso	£1.50 / £1.80
Cappuccino	£2.30 / £2.50
Latte	£2.30 / £2.50
Flat white	£2.30 / £2.50

RATING.

Fleet River Bakery

71 Lincoln's Inn Fields, WC2A 3JF

Tucked in the northwest corner of the beautiful Lincoln's Inn Fields, Fleet River Bakery is a good old-fashioned British bakery and kitchen that offers a wide range of sweet and savoury goods, all of which are made and prepared on-site each day. During the week, the ground-floor café quickly fills up at lunchtime, while the downstairs area offers a more peaceful space in which to enjoy your Monmouth coffee. Colourful photography adorns the walls and jars of sweets line the counter, enhancing the traditional British feel.

FOOD.

Breakfast, fresh sandwiches and a daily menu of salads, quiches and baked treats all made on site.

CONTACT.

+44(0)20 7691 1457
www.fleetriverbakery.com
info@fleetriverbakery.com
Holborn

OPEN.

Mon-Fri.	7:00am - 7:00pm
Sat.	9:00am - 5:00pm
Sun.	Closed

OVERVIEW.

Category
Bakery Coffee Shop
Owner
Jon Dalton
Head barista
Matilda, Ronnie and Stef
First opened
2009

COFFEE & EQUIPMENT.

Coffee roaster
Monmouth Coffee Company
Coffee machine
La Marzocco Linea, 3 groups
Coffee grinder
Anfim

COFFEE PRICING.

Espresso	£1.40 / £1.60
Cappuccino	£2.00 / £2.20
Latte	£2.00 / £2.20
Flat white	£2.00

RATING.

COFFEE 4.00 / 5

OVERALL 3.75 / 5

Ginger & White

4a-5a Perrins Court, NW3 1QS

OPEN.

Mon-Fri. 7:30am - 5:30pm
Sat-Sun. 8:30am - 5:30pm

This proudly British café wears its heart on its sleeve. A local gem that is ever-popular with the Hampstead community, Ginger & White serves well-crafted Square Mile coffee alongside modern British meals made using locally sourced produce. With the choice of a communal dining table, window seats or intimate leather sofas, this is a great place to enjoy a leisurely brunch.

FOOD.

Locally sourced British food - all-day breakfast, seasonal sarnies, fresh salads and homemade cakes.

CONTACT.

+44(0)20 7431 9098
www.gingerandwhite.com
info@gingerandwhite.com
Hampstead

OVERVIEW.

Category
Eatery
Owner
Tonia George, Nicholas and Emma Scott
Head barista
Van Lindsay
First opened
2009

COFFEE & EQUIPMENT.

Coffee roaster
Square Mile Coffee Roasters
Coffee machine
La Marzocco FB/80, 3 groups
Coffee grinder
Anfim, Mazzer Robur E

COFFEE PRICING.

Espresso	£1.80 / £2.00
Cappuccino	£2.40 / £2.70
Latte	£2.40 / £2.70
Flat white	£2.40 / £2.70

RATING.

COFFEE 4.25 / 5

OVERALL 4.25 / 5

Kipferl

20 Camden Passage, N1 8ED

OPEN.

Mon.	Closed
Tue.	9:00am - 6:00pm
Wed-Sat.	9:00am - 10:00pm
Sun.	10:00am - 6:00pm

After an image overhaul and a move to beautifully designed new premises in Angel, Kipferl is now a stylish venue offering the full traditional Viennese experience: coffee, cakes, strudel, soups, sausages and a full restaurant menu. The decor features muted grey, green and cream tones combined with timber panelling to create a warm, welcoming and peaceful space. Pop in for a melange and a rich Sachertorte for a real treat.

FOOD.

Traditional Austrian fare: specialty cakes such as Sachertorte and strudel, Viennese breakfast, soups, schnitzel, sausages and a full restaurant menu in the dining section.

CONTACT.

+44(0)20 7704 1555
www.kipferl.co.uk
mail@kipferl.co.uk
 Angel

Sister coffee shops.
Coram's Fields / Gordon Square

OVERVIEW.

Category
Bakery Coffee Shop
Owner
Christian Malnig
First opened
April 2011

COFFEE & EQUIPMENT.

Coffee roaster
Helmut Sachers
Coffee machine
Gaggia, 2 groups
Coffee grinder
Mazzer Mini

Coffee menu comprises **traditional Austrian coffees:** melange, brauner, verlangerter and schwarzer

COFFEE PRICING.

Espresso	£1.60 / £2.00
Cappuccino	£2.40
Latte	£2.70
Flat white (Melange)	£2.40 / £2.70 with cream

RATING.

COFFEE 3.75 / 5

OVERALL 4.00 / 5

Lanka

71 Regents Park Road, NW1 8UY

OPEN.

Tue-Fri. 9:00am - 6:30pm
Sat-Sun. 8:00am - 7:00pm
(Jan-March: Tue-Sat. 9:00am - 5:30pm, Sun. 9:00am - 5:00pm)

This delightful tea, coffee and cake house in Primrose Hill provides a lovely spot to sit and watch the well-heeled locals stroll by. Although small, the space is well utilised with a tantalising display of sweets and cakes, and an open frontage to make best use of the pavement tables. Laze away a Sunday afternoon with a coffee and a slice of green tea chocolate gateau for something a little different.

FOOD.

An intriguing combination of Japanese, French and British influences are evident in the breakfast, lunch and sweets menu.

CONTACT.

+44(0)20 7483 2544
www.lanka-uk.com
lanka@lanka-uk.com
Chalk Farm

OVERVIEW.

Category
Bakery Coffee Shop
Owner
Masayuki and Mina Hara
First opened
2010

COFFEE & EQUIPMENT.

Coffee roaster
Monmouth Coffee Company
Coffee machine
Stafco G10, 2 groups
Coffee grinder
Mazzer Super Jolly

COFFEE PRICING.

Espresso	£2.35
Cappuccino	£2.80
Latte	£2.80
Flat white	£2.80

RATING.

COFFEE 4.00 / 5
OVERALL 4.00 / 5

Leyas

20 Camden High Street, NW1 0JH

OPEN.

Mon-Fri. 7:30am - 6:30pm
Sat. 9:30am - 6:00pm
Sun. 9:30am - 5:30pm

Camden High Street has long been the domain of coffee chain outlets, but this independent newcomer provides a welcome alternative. Leyas was opened by cousins Leon and Yani in 2011 and is already a firm favourite with local office workers and residents. Delicious Union coffee is served to take away or enjoy in the inviting downstairs area where customers lounge on mismatched vintage chairs and sofas. Tasty sandwiches and free wifi makes this a great place to meet friends or colleagues for lunch and the cakes, made by a secret local supplier, are to die for.

FOOD.

Fresh and delicious sandwiches, bagels and salads. Cakes and pastries from an undisclosed local supplier. A strong contender for the best chocolate brownie in the city.

CONTACT.

www.leyas.co.uk
admin@leyas.co.uk
Mornington Crescent

OVERVIEW.

Category
Artisanal Independent
Owner
Yani Joseph and Leon Zadeh
First opened
September 2011

COFFEE & EQUIPMENT.

Coffee roaster
Union Hand-Roasted
Coffee machine
La Marzocco, 2 groups
Coffee grinder
Mazzer Super Jolly

COFFEE PRICING.

Espresso	£1.60
Cappuccino	£2.20
Latte	£2.20
Flat white	£2.20

RATING.

COFFEE 3.75 / 5

OVERALL 4.00 / 5

Look Mum No Hands!

49 Old Street, EC1V 9HX

Cycling is on the rise in London and Look Mum No Hands has rapidly become one of the city's busiest destinations for those who love bikes and coffee in equal measure. This lively cafe and bike workshop is decorated with bicycles, bike parts, Tour de France memorabilia, framed jerseys and flyers for events. The outdoor area is often filled with patrons enjoying a cup of Square Mile espresso or an alcoholic beverage and, during the Tour de France, this space is a full-on party zone. If you love bikes, coffee or both, Look Mum No Hands is an essential destination.

OPEN.

Mon-Fri. 7:00am - 10:00pm
Sat. 9:00am - 10:00pm
Sun. 10:00am - 10:00pm

OVERVIEW.

Category
Retail & Leisure
Owner
Sam Humpheson, Matthew Harper and Lewin Chalkley
Head barista
Jaanus Savisto
First opened
2010

COFFEE & EQUIPMENT.

Coffee roaster
Square Mile Coffee Roasters
Coffee machine
Faema Due, 2 groups and La Marzocco Linea, 2 groups
Coffee grinder
Anfim, Mazzer

COFFEE PRICING.

Espresso £1.60 / £1.90
Cappuccino £2.50
Latte £2.50
Flat white £2.30

FOOD.

Extensive breakfast and lunch menu including bacon sarnies, muffins, crumpets, salads, soups and pies. Plenty of vegetarian options.

CONTACT.

+44(0)20 7253 1025
www.lookmumnohands.com
info@lookmumnohands.com
Old Street

Also a **licensed bar** with a **wide selection of beers**

RATING.

COFFEE 4.25 / 5

OVERALL 4.25 / 5

Maison d'Etre

154 Canonbury Road, N1 2UP

OPEN.

Mon-Fri. 7.30am - 6:00pm
Sat-Sun. 10:00am - 6:00pm

This adorable new café on the Highbury roundabout is a labour of love for owners Kim and Kostas, who gave up their day jobs in 2010 to pursue a passion for food and coffee. Open since May 2011, Maison d'Etre serves Nude Espresso and a range of homemade cakes, sandwiches, treats and weekend brunch to an enthusiastic local crowd. Hand-painted murals, vintage china and a light, welcoming interior make this a serene spot to take five and sip a latte.

FOOD.

Homemade treats and sandwiches, fresh cakes and breads, and a weekend brunch menu.

CONTACT.

+44(0)20 7226 4711
www.maisondetrecafe.co.uk
hello@maisondetrecafe.co.uk
Highbury & Islington

OVERVIEW.

Category
Artisanal Independent
Owner
Kim Stephanie Kunn and Kostas Papakostas
First opened
May 2011

COFFEE & EQUIPMENT.

Coffee roaster
Nude Espresso
Coffee machine
La Marzocco Linea
Coffee grinder
Mazzer Super Jolly

COFFEE PRICING.

Espresso	£1.80
Cappuccino	£2.20
Latte	£2.20
Flat white	£2.20

RATING.

COFFEE 4.25 / 5

OVERALL 4.00 / 5

Melrose & Morgan Primrose Hill

42 Gloucester Avenue, NW1 8JD

OPEN.

Mon-Fri.	8:00am - 5:00pm
Sat.	8:00am - 5:00pm
Sun.	9:00am - 4:00pm

This grocer and deli in leafy Primrose Hill is a cornucopia of beautifully presented and locally sourced food. Homemade preserves fill the shelves, while a daily selection of seasonal salads, sandwiches, soups, cakes and treats are laid out on a broad wooden table in the centre of the store. Breads and vegetables are also available, along with artisanal foods and a range of gourmet readymade meals. The coffee machine lives in the kitchen, adjacent to a small window bar area where customers can sip espresso in the sunshine.

FOOD.

A tempting array of salads, quiches and pastries, plus cheeses, chutney, ready meals and wine to take away.

CONTACT.

+44(0)20 7722 0011
www.melroseandmorgan
info@melroseandmorgan.com

Sister coffee shops.
Hampstead

OVERVIEW.

Category
Eatery
Owner
Nick Selby and Ian James
First opened
2004

COFFEE & EQUIPMENT.

Coffee roaster
Climpson & Sons
Coffee machine
La Marzocco Linea, 2 groups
Coffee grinder
Anfim

COFFEE PRICING.

Espresso	£1.60 / £1.85
Cappuccino	£2.40
Latte	£2.40
Flat white	£2.40

RATING.

COFFEE 4.25 / 5

OVERALL 3.75 / 5

Ottolenghi Islington

287 Upper Street, N1 2TZ

The outstanding food presentation at Ottolenghi makes this venue a feast for the eyes, as well as the taste buds. Piles of giant meringues, stacks of cakes, trays of fresh salads and an array of savouries create an irresistible display at the front of this well-known eatery, and customers awaiting a table have ample opportunity to eye up their options. Communal tables and sleek, modern design make the interior vibrant and social and Ottolenghi remains busy from morning until evening. As the conclusion to a memorable brunch, lunch or special dinner, Square Mile coffee is the perfect digestif.

Sister coffee shops.
Notting Hill / Kensington / Belgravia

TOP 30

Images supplied by Ottolenghi

OPEN.

Mon-Sat. 8:00am - 11:00pm
Sun. 9:00am - 7:00pm

OVERVIEW.

Category
Eatery
Owner
Yotam Ottolenghi
First opened
2004

COFFEE & EQUIPMENT.

Coffee roaster
Square Mile Coffee Roasters
Coffee machine
La Marzocco Linea, 3 groups
Coffee grinder
Anfim

COFFEE PRICING.

Espresso	£2.35
Cappuccino	£2.50 / £3.00
Latte	£2.50 / £3.00
Flat white	£2.50 / £3.00

FOOD.

Breakfast, lunch, dinner and everything in between, all freshly made on site and beautifully displayed.

CONTACT.

+44(0)20 7288 1454
www.ottolenghi.co.uk
upper@ottolenghi.co.uk
Highbury & Islington

RATING.

Sacred Highbury Studios

8 Hornsey Street, N7 8EG

Located in the Highbury Studios complex among office buildings and close to London Metropolitan University, this spacious café continues with the New Zealand theme consistent across Sacred's other locations. Plenty of comfy couches and quiet nooks are available where customers can kick back and enjoy a coffee, while food for all Sacred stores is produced in the generous kitchen.

Sister coffee shops.
Ganton Street / Covent Garden / Westfield London / Kingly Court / Torrington Street

OPEN.

Mon-Fri. 7:30am - 6:00pm
Sat. 9:00am - 5:00pm
Sun. 9:00am - 4:00pm

OVERVIEW.

Category
Chain
Owner
Tubbs Wanigasekera and Matt Clark
Head barista
Prue Randall
First opened
2009

COFFEE & EQUIPMENT.

Coffee roaster
Sacred House Roast
Coffee machine
La Marzocco Linea, 2 groups
Coffee grinder
Mazzer Robur

COFFEE PRICING.

Espresso	£1.60
Cappuccino	£2.50 / £2.70
Latte	£2.50 / £2.70
Flat white	£2.50 / £2.70

FOOD.

Full breakfast, Kiwi-style brunch and lunch menu all cooked fresh on site.

CONTACT.

+44(0)20 7700 1628
www.sacredcafe.co.uk
globalcoffee@gmail.com
Holloway Road

Tinderbox

N1 Centre, Parkfield Street, N1 0PS

Image supplied by Tinderbox

OPEN.

Mon-Fri. 6:30am - 10:30pm
Sat-Sun. 8:00am - 10:30pm

Deceptively small on the ground floor, Tinderbox has much more to offer than may be apparent at first glance. The downstairs espresso bar is for takeaway only, so head up the wooden staircase to discover a large café with plenty of seating. Prized spots are the warm booths where customers can enjoy an Algie coffee or meet friends before seeing a film at the nearby cinema. Family-owned Tinderbox combines the professionalism of a chain with the charm of an independent.

FOOD.

Sandwiches, snacks, cakes and treats for any time of day.

CONTACT.

+44(0)20 7354 8929
tinderbox.upper@gmail.com
Angel

Sister coffee shops.
Spitalfields / Westfield Stratford / four in Scotland

OVERVIEW.

Category
Artisanal Independent
Owner
Carlo Ventisei
Head barista
Guido Gessarolli
First opened
2009

COFFEE & EQUIPMENT.

Coffee roaster
Matthew Algie
Coffee machine
Elektra Barlume, 3 groups
Coffee grinder
Mazzer x2

COFFEE PRICING.

Espresso £1.80 / £2.20
Cappuccino £2.10 / £2.50 / £2.90
Latte £2.50 / £2.90
Flat white £2.50

RATING.

Wild & Wood Coffee

1-19 New Oxford Street, WC1A 1BA

Image supplied by Wild and Wood

OPEN.

Mon-Fri.	7:30am - 5:45pm
Sat.	10:00am - 5:30pm
Sun.	10:00am - 3:00pm

Open for more than 30 years, Wild & Wood is one of the oldest coffee shops in the central London area and has become a Farringdon institution. The small interior has a warm and cosy feel, with wood panelling throughout, old church pew seats and an intimate seating nook. Classic photographs of beloved British TV characters and old-school rock 'n' roll music add to the authentic charm of this popular café, and Monmouth coffee is served at some of the most reasonable prices in town.

FOOD.

An appetising array of pastries, sandwiches and cakes are nicely displayed by the window.

CONTACT.

+44(0)75 2515 5957
wildwoodbean@yahoo.com
Holborn

OVERVIEW.

Category
Artisanal Independent
Owner / head barista
Bozena Mazerant
First opened
1978

COFFEE & EQUIPMENT.

Coffee roaster
Monmouth Coffee Company
Coffee machine
La Spaziale, 2 groups
Coffee grinder
Mazzer Luigi

COFFEE PRICING.

Espresso	£2.20
Cappuccino	£2.20
Latte	£2.20
Flat white	£2.20

Single-origin filter coffee is also available

RATING.

COFFEE 4.25 / 5

OVERALL 4.00 / 5

The 3 Little Pigs at Black Truffle

52 Warren Street, W1T 5NJ

This unique kiosk inside the Black Truffle shoe and accessories shop is one of London's best-kept coffee secrets. Take a turn off bustling Tottenham Court Road and join a select crowd of in-the-know regulars who can be found sipping Nude espresso while browsing the shoes and bags or munching a toasted bagel at the bar. Shoemaking classes are also available at the Prescott & Mackay workshop downstairs.

OPEN.

Mon-Fri. 8:00am - 3:00pm

Owner
Michael Needham

COFFEE & EQUIPMENT.

Coffee roaster
Nude Espresso
Coffee machine
Faema E61
Coffee grinder
Mazzer x 2

Coleman Coffee

55 Stanworth Street, SE1 3NY

Alongside a range of artisanal food suppliers including brewers, bakers and cheesemakers, up-and-coming coffee roaster Jack Coleman serves his unique coffee blends to queues of customers who travel to Maltby Street on Saturdays for their cup of batch-roasted black gold. Piles of fresh, fragrant coffee beans displayed in bowls can be scooped into bags to take home or ground and brewed on the spot for a filter coffee fix.

OPEN.
Sat. only 8:30am - 3:00pm

Owner
Jack Coleman

COFFEE & EQUIPMENT.

Coffee roaster
Coleman Coffee
Coffee machine
La Marzocco Linea, 2 groups
Coffee grinder
Mazzer Super Jolly 1970

Dark Fluid

Brockley Market, Lewisham College Car Park, Lewisham Way, SE4 1UT

Dark Fluid is the new incarnation of popular market stall Exchange Coffee, which has now blossomed into an award-winning boutique roastery and coffee vendor at Brockley Market. South London locals flock here each week for unique espresso blends and single-origin beans that have been hand-roasted by passionate coffee-head Lawrence Sinclair, as well as to enjoy the wealth of fresh food and produce on offer at this, one of London's most enjoyable markets.

OPEN.
Sat. only 10:00am - 2:00pm

Owner
Lawrence Sinclair

COFFEE & EQUIPMENT.

Coffee roaster
Dark Fluid
Coffee machine
Kees van der Westen Mirage
Coffee grinder
Mazzer

Flat Cap Coffee Co

4 Strutton Ground (SW1P 2HR), Borough Market (SE1 1TL) and Fleet St (EC4A 2HR)

The polished wagons of Flat Cap Coffee can be found dispensing fresh Square Mile espresso at three locations: Strutton Ground in Westminster, Borough Market and on the corner of Fleet Street and Fetter Lane. Owned by well-respected coffee barons Robert and Fabio of Notes Music & Coffee, the Flat Cap carts are always a welcome sight around London and are synonymous with quality street coffee.

Owner
Robert Robinson and Fabio Ferreira

OPEN.

Strutton Ground:
Mon-Fri. 8:00am - 4:30pm

Borough Market:
Thu. 11:00am - 5:00pm
Fri. 12:00pm - 6:00pm
Sat. 8:00am - 5:00pm

Corner of Fleet St & Fetter Lane:
Mon-Fri. 8:00am - 4:30pm

COFFEE & EQUIPMENT.

Coffee roaster
Square Mile Coffee Roasters
Coffee machine
La Marzocco GB/5 and FB/80
Coffee grinder
Anfim Super Caimano

Giddy Up

Fortune Street Park (EC1Y) and 93 Great Eastern Street (EC2A 3JD)

Just around the corner from the famous Whitecross Street Market is Fortune Street Park, a charming patch of green in the backstreets of Barbican that now hosts one of the best coffee carts in London. Owner Lee Harte's barista street-smarts were honed at the Pitch 42, Columbia Road and Flat Cap coffee stalls. This expertise is evident in the attention to detail found here and at Giddy Up Floripa - a second stall located at the top of Paul Street and equipped with a Kees van der Westen Mirage.

Owner
Lee Harte

OPEN.

Fortune Street Park:
Mon-Fri. 8:00am - 4:30pm
Sat-Sun. 10:00am - 4:00pm

Paul Street:
Mon-Fri. 7:00am - 4:00pm
Sat-Sun. 10:00am - 4:00pm

COFFEE & EQUIPMENT.

Coffee roaster
Square Mile Coffee Roasters, Has Bean
Coffee machine
La Marzocco GB40, 2 groups, Kees van der Westen Mirage
Coffee grinder
Anfim, Mazzer

Merito Coffee

Eton Avenue (NW3 3EP) and Broadway Market (E8 4PH)

Bringing consistently excellent espresso to the markets of London since 2007, Merito Coffee is a welcome constant in an ever-changing London coffee landscape. Operating at the Swiss Cottage Market three days a week and the heaving Broadway Market on Saturdays, owner Jason Fitzpatrick and barista Ian Cameron use both an espresso machine and drip filters to make some of London's best coffee for their loyal coterie of customers. Several varieties are also available for purchase.

OPEN.

Swiss Cottage:
Wed-Fri. 8:00am - 3:00pm

Broadway Market:
Sat. 8.30am - 4:00pm

Owner
Jason Fitzpatrick

COFFEE & EQUIPMENT.

Coffee roaster
Various
Coffee machine
Caffe Izzo, 2 groups
Coffee grinder
Mazzer

Nomad Espresso

Netil Market, 11-25 Westgate Street, E8 3RL

Nomad baristas Asher and Jordi run their coffee cart "off Broadway" at Netil Market – the quirkier, more bohemian cousin of the famous Broadway Market around the corner. Pulling a mean Square Mile espresso through their shiny new Wega, these skilled young baristas do a roaring trade alongside a range of food and vintage stalls on Saturdays. Take a stroll off the beaten track and be rewarded with superb coffee and friendly smiles.

OPEN.

Sat. only 10:00am - 6:00pm

Owner
Asher Preston and Jordi Mestre

COFFEE & EQUIPMENT.

Coffee roaster
Square Mile Coffee Roasters
Coffee machine
Wega, 2 groups
Coffee grinder
Mazzer

Prufrock at Present

140 Shoreditch High Street, E1 6JE

Located inside designer men's clothing store Present on Shoreditch High Street, this outpost of Prufrock Coffee is a place to be seen, as well as to enjoy impeccable coffee alongside the fashionistas, artists and creatives of Shoreditch. At the coffee bar by the door, award-winning baristas use a glittering manual Victoria Arduino to extract some of London's best espresso for this stylish crowd.

OPEN.

Mon-Fri.	10:30am - 7:00pm
Sat.	11:00am - 6:00pm
Sun.	11:00am - 5:00pm

Owner
Gwilym Davies and Jeremy Challender

COFFEE & EQUIPMENT.

Coffee roaster
Square Mile Coffee Roasters

Coffee machine
Victoria Arduino Athena Leva, 2 groups

Coffee grinder
Nuova Simonelli Mythos

Pitch 42 at Whitecross St Market

Whitecross Street Market, EC1Y 8JL

In recent years, Pitch 42 at Whitecross Street Market has become renowned as a hotbed of coffee experimentation and espresso excellence, producing barista champions and a new generation of London coffee thought leaders. Now operating under new ownership, Pitch 42 remains a worthwhile coffee destination, not least for its location at the eclectic Whitecross Street lunchtime market.

OPEN.

Mon-Fri. 8:00am - 2:30pm

Owner
Stephan Vital-Barette

COFFEE & EQUIPMENT.

Coffee roaster
Square Mile Coffee Roasters

Coffee machine
Brugnetti

Coffee grinder
Anfim

The Sandwich & the Spoon

Bridge Approach, NW1 8BE

Tucked away at one end of a picturesque pedestrian bridge in Primrose Hill is The Sandwich & the Spoon, a new coffee cart manned by barista and graphic designer Gavin Fernback. Quirky magnets and index cards adorn Fernback's La Marzocco, his takeaway cups are hand-stamped with a sandwich + spoon logo and the blackboard sign that announces his cart's presence on Bridge Approach has already become legendary for its irreverent messages. Along with a rotating menu of coffee beans, Gavin sells bottles of single-herd organic milk and cakes and biscuits baked by his mum.

OPEN.

Mon-Fri. 7:30am - 3:00pm

Owner
Gavin Fernback

COFFEE & EQUIPMENT.

Coffee roaster
Various

Coffee machine
La Marzocco Linea, 2 groups

Coffee grinder
Anfim

Inner East

Brick Lane and Shoreditch provide London's creative pulse and are areas of tremendous diversity that have undergone rapid change in recent years. Many of the city's best new roasteries are based in East London and a range of artisan coffee venues provide fuel for the artists, students and urbanites that flock here for the weekend markets.

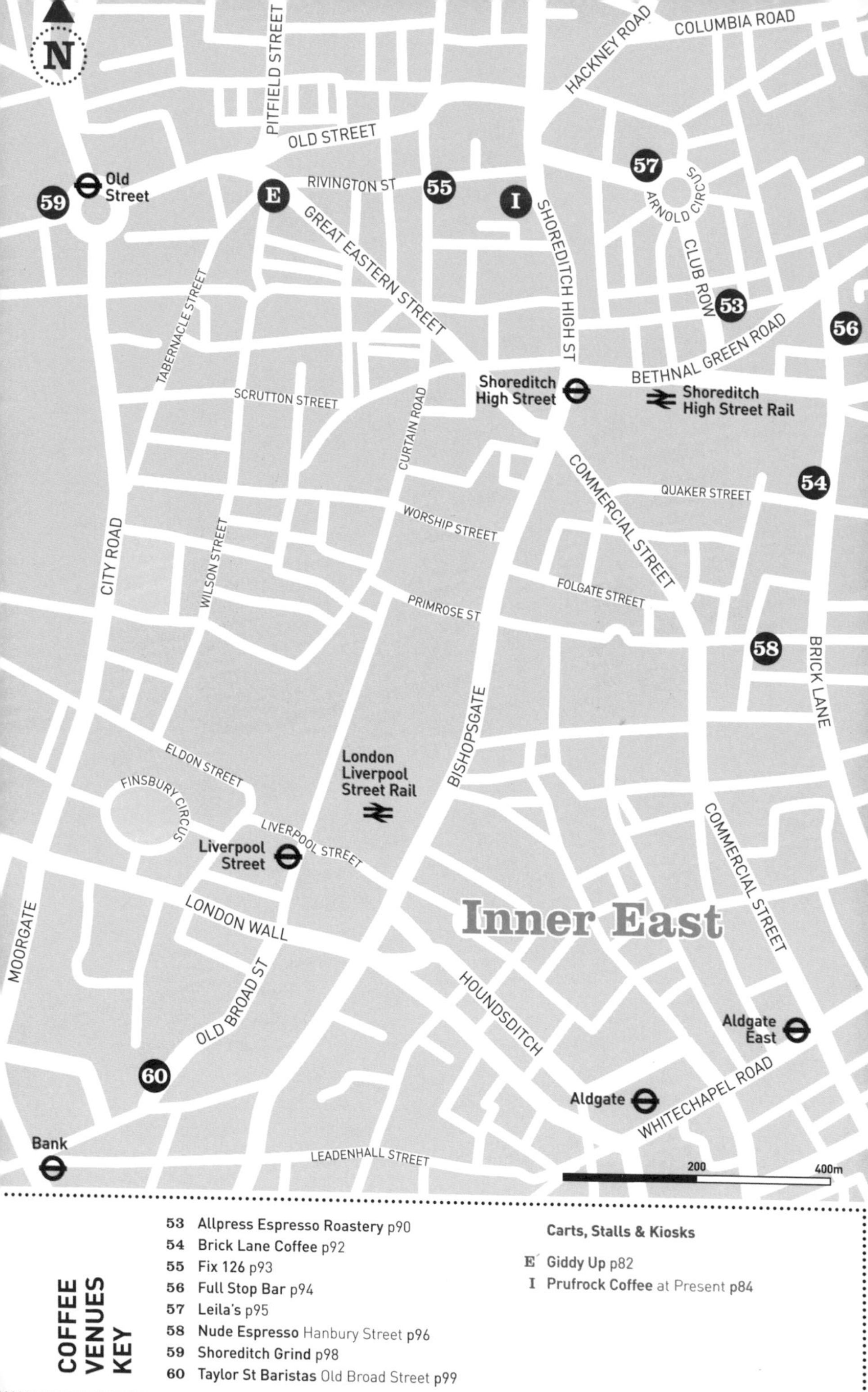
N
HACKNEY ROAD
COLUMBIA ROAD
PITFIELD STREET
OLD STREET
Old Street
59
E
RIVINGTON ST
55
I
57
ARNOLD CIRCUS
SHOREDITCH HIGH ST
GREAT EASTERN STREET
CLUB ROW
53
56
TABERNACLE STREET
BETHNAL GREEN ROAD
Shoreditch High Street
Shoreditch High Street Rail
SCRUTTON STREET
CURTAIN ROAD
COMMERCIAL STREET
QUAKER STREET
54
WORSHIP STREET
CITY ROAD
WILSON STREET
FOLGATE STREET
PRIMROSE ST
58
BRICK LANE
BISHOPSGATE
ELDON STREET
London Liverpool Street Rail
FINSBURY CIRCUS
Liverpool Street
LIVERPOOL STREET
LONDON WALL
Inner East
COMMERCIAL STREET
MOORGATE
OLD BROAD ST
HOUNDSDITCH
Aldgate East
60
Aldgate
WHITECHAPEL ROAD
Bank
LEADENHALL STREET
200
400m
COFFEE VENUES KEY
53 Allpress Espresso Roastery p90
54 Brick Lane Coffee p92
55 Fix 126 p93
56 Full Stop Bar p94
57 Leila's p95
58 Nude Espresso Hanbury Street p96
59 Shoreditch Grind p98
60 Taylor St Baristas Old Broad Street p99
Carts, Stalls & Kiosks
E Giddy Up p82
I Prufrock Coffee at Present p84

Allpress Espresso Roastery

58 Redchurch Street, E2 7DJ

This first UK venue for well-established New Zealand roastery Allpress Espresso has rapidly become a firm favourite in the heart of Shoreditch. The café's simple, natural interior focuses attention on the coffee itself - a gleaming roaster is proudly on display and coffee expertise is evident in every detail of this space. Allpress has had huge success in New Zealand and Australia, supplying many coffee shops and high-end restaurants on both sides of the Tasman. Since its opening just over a year ago, Allpress has thrown out a challenge to the UK market and coffee lovers have reaped the rewards, with a host of new ventures mimicking this highly popular model.

Image supplied by Allpress Espresso Roastery

OPEN.

Mon-Fri. 8:00am - 5:00pm
Sat-Sun. 9:00am - 5:00pm

OVERVIEW.

Category
Artisanal Independent

Owner
Michael Allpress and Tony Papas

First opened
2010

COFFEE & EQUIPMENT.

Coffee roaster
Allpress

Coffee machine
La Marzocco Strada, 3 groups

Coffee grinder
Mazzer Robur, Mazzer Super Jolly, Mahlkönig, Marco Über Boiler

COFFEE PRICING.

Espresso	£2.00
Cappuccino	£2.50
Latte	£2.50
Flat white	£2.50

FOOD.

A selection of Italian sandwiches, pastries, cakes and light brunch dishes.

CONTACT.

+44(0)20 7749 1780
www.allpressespresso.com
coffee@allpress.co.uk
Shoreditch High Street

Filter pourovers are available and **coffee roasting is carried out on site**

RATING.

COFFEE 4.50 / 5

OVERALL 4.50 / 5

Brick Lane Coffee

157 Brick Lane, E1 6SB

OPEN.

Daily: 7:00am - 8:00pm

Situated at the northern end of Brick Lane, this headquarters for the Street Coffee chain oozes alternative cool. The mish-mash of vintage furniture, eclectic wall art featuring pop-cultural icons and the bicycles crammed inside create a youthful, urban feel. Art students and East London locals linger on the couches, except on Sundays when Brick Lane Market turns this café into a heaving hub for bargain hunters. If you're not in the mood for a coffee, the smoothies and frappés are also a popular alternative.

FOOD.

A selection of sandwiches, soups and snacks.

CONTACT.

+44(0)20 7729 2667
www.streetcoffee.co.uk

Shoreditch High Street

Sister coffee shops.
Goswell Road / Bermondsey Street

OVERVIEW.

Category
Chain

Owner
Street Coffee / Adrian Jones

First opened
2001

COFFEE & EQUIPMENT.

Coffee roaster
Ethica Coffee

Coffee machine
Rancilio Classe 8, 3 groups

Coffee grinder
Mazzer Super Jolly, Mazzer Mini

COFFEE PRICING.

Espresso	£1.70
Cappuccino	£2.20 / £2.50 / £2.80
Latte	£2.00 / £2.35 / £2.70
Flat white	£2.30 / £2.50

RATING.

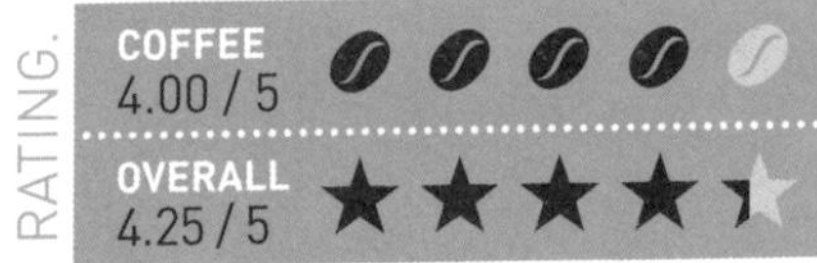

Fix 126

126 Curtain Road, EC2A 3PJ

OPEN.

Mon-Fri.	7:00am - 7:00pm
Sat-Sun.	8:00am - 7:00pm

This second Fix location in Shoreditch is a hub of creativity and a popular place for locals to meet up and collaborate, or simply work alone on their laptops or sketchbooks. This is also an excellent spot to stop for a daily caffeine fix, and friendly staff are happy to chat while whipping up a custom-blended cup of Fix 126 Climpson's espresso. A seat at one of the large front windows is an ideal place to sit and observe the comings and goings along vibrant Curtain Road.

FOOD.

A fresh range of takeaway lunch options, snacks and a tempting variety of baked treats.

CONTACT.

+44(0)20 7033 9555
fix-coffee.co.uk
info@fix-coffee.co.uk
Shoreditch High Street

Sister coffee shops.
Fix (Whitecross Street)

OVERVIEW.

Category
Artisanal Independent
Owner
Sasha Rainey
First opened
July 2011

COFFEE & EQUIPMENT.

Coffee roaster
Climpson & Sons
Coffee machine
La Marzocco GB/5, 3 groups
Coffee grinder
Mazzer Robur E, Mazzer Super Jolly

COFFEE PRICING.

Espresso	£1.50 / £2.00
Cappuccino	£2.40 / £2.60
Latte	£2.40 / £2.60
Flat white	£2.40

RATING.

COFFEE 4.25 / 5

OVERALL 4.00 / 5

Full Stop

202 Brick Lane, E1 6SA

OPEN.

Mon-Thu.	8:00am - 11:00pm
Fri.	8:00am - 12:30am
Sat.	9:00am - 12:30am
Sun.	9:00am - 11:00pm

West London's popular Indie Coffee cart has reinvented itself as Full Stop, a cosy hangout across the other side of town on Brick Lane. Fittingly for its location, a vintage aesthetic predominates at Full Stop, with bench seats, Formica tables and comfy sofas furnishing a long, cosy space. However, the offering at Full Stop is far from antique, with fresh gourmet sandwiches and cakes providing the perfect complement to expertly prepared Square Mile espresso. Owner Peter Duggan's old Indie Coffee cart can still be found in the hallway and will soon serve takeaway beverages at the front door.

FOOD.

Pastries by Seven Seeded and cakes baked on-site. Gourmet sandwiches.

CONTACT.

Shoreditch High Street

OVERVIEW.

Category
Artisanal Independent

Owner / Head barista
Peter Duggan

First opened
October 2011

COFFEE & EQUIPMENT.

Coffee roaster
Square Mile Coffee Roasters

Coffee machine
La Marzocco Linea, 2 groups

Coffee grinder
Mazzer, Anfim

COFFEE PRICING.

Espresso	£2.00
Cappuccino	£2.50
Latte	£2.50
Flat white	£2.50

A delicious **range of posh hot chocolates** is also available

RATING.

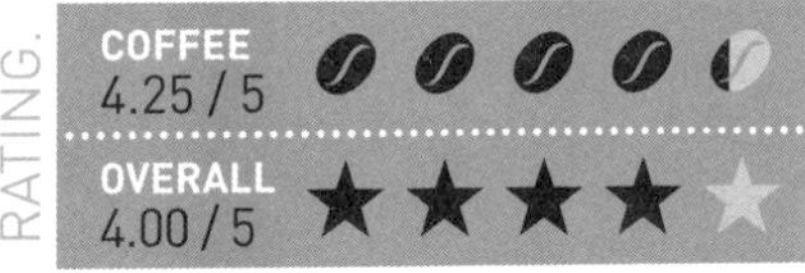

Leila's

17 Calvert Avenue, E2 7JP

OPEN.

Mon-Tue.	Closed
Wed-Sat.	10:00am - 6:00pm
Sun.	10:00am - 5:00pm

Leila's combines a country kitchen with a local café to create one of Shoreditch's cosiest and most appealing venues. The Leila's Shop deli sells a wide range of produce from fruit and veg to preserves and pasta, while the café next door offers simple but beautifully prepared breakfasts and lunches to East Londoners looking for something more authentic than the usual painfully hip fare. Like the food, the coffee is also fresh, good and prepared with care.

FOOD.

A daily menu of soups, sandwiches and homemade treats.

CONTACT.

+44(0)20 7729 9789
info@leilasshop.com
Shoreditch High Street

OVERVIEW.

Category
Artisanal Independent
Owner
Leila McAlister
First opened
2002

COFFEE & EQUIPMENT.

Coffee roaster
Coleman Coffee
Coffee machine
La Marzocco Linea, 2 groups
Coffee grinder
Mazzer Luigi

COFFEE PRICING.

Espresso	£2.00
Cappuccino	£2.50
Latte	£2.50
Flat white	£2.50

RATING.

COFFEE 4.00 / 5

OVERALL 4.00 / 5

Nude Espresso

26 Hanbury Street, E1 6QR

Located close to the bustling Spitalfields market on Saturdays and Brick Lane market on Sundays, Nude Espresso is one of London's busiest weekend destinations for food and coffee lovers. However, Nude offers much more than just a pit stop for weekend shoppers, with its famous East espresso blend and a full menu of brewing options making it well worth braving the mobs any day of the week. The Nude Espresso Roastery itself is just around the corner on Brick Lane and is open Thursday to Saturday for anyone who wants to learn more about the coffee-making process.

TOP 30

COFFEE PRICING.

Espresso £2.00
Cappuccino £2.50
Latte £2.50
Flat white £2.50

FOOD.

An appetising Antipodean-style breakfast and brunch menu and tempting display of salads and baked goods.

CONTACT.

+44(0)78 0422 3590
www.nudeespresso.com
rich@nudeespresso.com
Shoreditch High Street

OPEN.

Mon-Fri. 7:30am - 6:00pm
Sat-Sun. 10:00am - 6:00pm

OVERVIEW.

Category
Artisanal Independent

Owner
Richard Reed

Head barista
Kurtis Leigh

First opened
2008

COFFEE & EQUIPMENT.

Coffee roaster
Nude Espresso

Coffee machine
Modified Wega Nova, 3 groups

Coffee grinder
Wega Compak K10 x 3

Sister coffee shops.
Soho Square /
Brick Lane (Roastery)

RATING.

COFFEE 4.50 / 5

OVERALL 4.50 / 5

Shoreditch Grind

213 Old Street, EC1V 9NR

OPEN.

Mon-Fri.	7:00am - 8:00pm
Sat.	9:00am - 6:00pm
Sun.	10:00am - 6:00pm

With its retro cinema signage, circular interior and prime location right on the Old Street "Silicon" roundabout, Shoreditch Grind is coffee theatre at its finest. Coffee lovers can sit on bar stools and look out at one of the city's busiest transport hubs while feeling insulated from the rat race with a cup of the delicious house blend in hand. Big things are planned for this popular new venue, with an upstairs recording studio, an expanded menu and more seating areas on the cards for 2012.

FOOD.

Sandwiches, cakes, pastries, salads and hot food. Chocolates and peppermints are also sold on the counter.

CONTACT.

+44(0)20 7490 7490
www.shoreditchgrind.com
info@shoreditchgrind.com
Shoreditch High Street

OVERVIEW.

Category
Artisanal Independent
Owner
Kaz James and David Abrahamovitch
Head barista
Tobin Ventham
First opened
June 2011

COFFEE & EQUIPMENT.

Coffee roaster
Shoreditch Grind house blend
Coffee machine
La Marzocco, 3 groups
Coffee grinder
Mazzer

COFFEE PRICING.

Espresso	£1.95
Cappuccino	£2.45 / £2.75
Latte	£2.45 / £2.75
Flat white	£2.45 / £2.75

RATING.

COFFEE 4.25 / 5

OVERALL 4.25 / 5

Taylor St Baristas Old Broad St

125 Old Broad Street, EC2N 1AR

Taylor Street Baristas' Bank venue is the largest and busiest café in its rapidly growing family of venues. The sleek and spacious design includes lofty ceilings, timber finishings and designer drop lights that make this a great place for a business meeting or lunchtime escape. The daily menu is projected onto the wall behind the bar and includes a rotating range of fresh, Antipodean-style food.

FOOD.

Delicious fresh salads, sandwiches, soups and more made on site daily.

CONTACT.

+44(0)79 8158 9484
www.taylor-st.com
info@taylor-st.com
Bank

Sister coffee shops.
Six other locations in London and Brighton

OPEN.

Mon-Fri.	7:00am - 5:00pm
Sat-Sun.	Closed

OVERVIEW.

Category
Artisanal Independent

Owner
Nick, Andrew and Laura Tolley

Head barista
Andrew Tolley

First opened
2010

COFFEE & EQUIPMENT.

Coffee roaster
Union Hand-Roasted

Coffee machine
Nuova Simonelli Aurelia, 3 groups and Synesso Hydra, 3 groups

Coffee grinder
Anfim Super Caimano x 3, Mazzer Robur E x 2, Ditting

COFFEE PRICING.

Espresso	£1.20 / £1.40
Cappuccino	£2.40 / £2.60 / £3.10
Latte	£2.40 / £2.60 / £3.10
Flat white	£2.40 / £3.00 / £3.50

RATING.

COFFEE 4.50 / 5

OVERALL 4.25 / 5

Hackney

Hackney has successfully shaken its label as a rough outer region to emerge as London's booming artistic neighbourhood. A wonderful combination of cultures and a thriving creative scene have helped put Hackney back on the map. The world's attention will be on the area during the 2012 Olympics, providing an excellent opportunity for new coffee venues to make their mark.

Betty's Coffee

510b Kingsland Road, E8 4AE

OPEN.

Mon-Fri.	8:00am - 8:00pm
Sat.	10:00am - 8:00pm
Sun.	10:00am - 6:00pm

This small but cosy café on Kingsland Road has quickly become a favourite with Dalston locals for its bohemian community feel, friendly baristas and delicious Allpress coffee. The rustic wood and exposed brick interior is complemented by Turkish cushions, a generously stocked bookshelf and an interactive mural, and hidden out the back is a pleasant outdoor area. Design-your-own paninis, sandwiches, bagels and homemade cakes round out the food offer and make Betty's a perfect lunchtime pit stop.

FOOD.

A range of paninis, sandwiches, bagels and homemade cakes.

CONTACT.

www.bettyscoffee.co.uk
info@bettyscoffee.co.uk
Dalston Junction

OVERVIEW.

Category
Artisanal Independent
Owner
Bethany Sharpe
Head barista
Rapunzel
First opened
April 2011

COFFEE & EQUIPMENT.

Coffee roaster
Allpress
Coffee machine
La Marzocco, 2 groups
Coffee grinder
Mazzer

COFFEE PRICING.

Espresso	£1.50
Cappuccino	£2.10
Latte	£2.10
Flat white	£2.10

RATING.

COFFEE
4.25 / 5

OVERALL
4.00 / 5

Cà Phê VN (Saigon Street Cafe)

Broadway Market, E8 4PH

OPEN.

Sat. only 10:00am - 5:00pm

(Closed January)

If you like your coffee strong, this is the place for you. Occupying a corner stall of Hackney's Broadway Market every Saturday, Cá Phê VN provides a Vietnamese-style caffeine hit like no other in London. Relax in a canvas deck chair and enjoy a heart-starting iced coffee (a summer specialty) as the eclectic market crowd strolls by. Husband-and-wife team Rob Atthill and Tuyen Hong source their coffee directly from farmers in Vietnam and also sell wholesale to numerous suppliers and restaurants across the UK.

FOOD.

Try Cá Phê VN's celebrated pork baguette, its version of typical Vietnamese street food.

CONTACT.

+44(0)77 8078 4696
www.caphevn.co.uk
caphevn@aol.com
Bethnal Green

Also serve **Vietnamese iced coffee -** £2.00

OVERVIEW.

Category
Stall / Cart / Kiosk
Owner
Rob Atthill and Tuyen Hong
Head barista
Khoa Nguyen
First opened
2007

COFFEE & EQUIPMENT.

Coffee roaster
Cà Phê VN
Coffee machine
Drip filter

COFFEE PRICING.

All coffees £1.50 - Vietnamese specialties, either black or sweetened with condensed milk

Sister coffee shops.
Clerkenwell Road / Upper Street

RATING.

COFFEE 4.00 / 5

OVERALL 3.75 / 5

Climpson & Sons

67 Broadway Market, E8 4PH

Revered by coffee lovers in East London and beyond, the Climpson & Sons café and roastery has developed into one of the biggest names in London coffee. You'll be lucky to even make it through the door of the café while Broadway Market is in full swing on Saturday and the seats outside are always packed, but luckily the same team operates a stall at the southern end of the market to help meet demand. The Climpsons roastery is located just up the road and supplies its roasts to a fast-growing number of London's best cafés and restaurants. A variety of blends are also available for purchase at the café.

OPEN.

Mon-Fri.	8:00am - 5:00pm
Sat.	8:30am - 5:00pm
Sun.	9:00am - 4:00pm

OVERVIEW.

Category
Artisanal Independent
Owner
Ian Burgess
Head barista
Danny Davies
First opened
2004

COFFEE & EQUIPMENT.

Coffee roaster
Climpson & Sons
Coffee machine
La Marzocco Linea, 3 groups
Coffee grinder
Mazzer

Sister coffee shops.
Climpson & Sons Broadway
Market stall (Saturdays)

Climpson & Sons **roasts its own beans** at a roastery just up the road

COFFEE PRICING.

Espresso	£1.60
Cappuccino	£2.20 / £2.40
Latte	£2.20 / £2.40
Flat white	£2.20 / £2.40

FOOD.

Breakfast dishes, sandwiches, pies, soups and grilled toasts are made with produce sourced from local businesses.

CONTACT.

+44(0)20 7812 9829
www.climpsonandsons.com
Bethnal Green

RATING.

COFFEE 4.50 / 5

OVERALL 4.50 / 5

The Container Café

View Tube, Stratford, E15 2PJ

OPEN.

Daily: 9:00am - 5:00pm

(The Container Café will be closed from May 23 until after the conclusion of the 2012 Olympic Games)

Located at the heart of the London Olympic site in the View Tube building, the Container Café is a unique coffee experience. The café space is laidback, with a communal table, retro furniture and comfortable lounge seats, while the large windows and outdoor tables provide the perfect vantage point to see the Olympic site in all its glory. Great coffee and scrumptious food are consistent with sister café The Counter, which is just a short walk away.

FOOD.

Freshly made breakfast, bagels, soups and sandwiches. Try the delicious bacon baguette with homemade relish.

CONTACT.

+44(0)78 3427 5687
www.theviewtube.co.uk
info@thecountercafe.co.uk
Hackney Wick

Sister coffee shops.
The Counter Café

OVERVIEW.

Category
Artisanal Independent
Owner
Tom and Jess Seaton
Head barista
Ronni Painter
First opened
2009

COFFEE & EQUIPMENT.

Coffee roaster
Square Mile Coffee Roasters
Coffee machine
La Marzocco Linea, 2 groups
Coffee grinder
Anfim

COFFEE PRICING.

Espresso	£1.40
Cappuccino	£2.00
Latte	£2.50
Flat white	£2.00

RATING.

COFFEE 4.25 / 5

OVERALL 4.25 / 5

The Counter Café

TOP 30

Stour Space, 7 Roach Road, E3 2PA

OPEN.

Mon-Fri. 7:45am - 5:00pm
Sat-Sun. 9:00am - 5:00pm

Open for tapas:
Thu-Sun. 6:30pm - late

The Counter Café has new premises inside the Stour Space gallery, just a few doors down from its old digs on Roach Road. The change is for the better - the new-look Counter is lighter and more spacious with added seating and a gorgeous view directly onto the canal. The grungy look of the old space hasn't been lost, with smashed brick walls and the cafe's signature vintage cinema seats ensuring these shiny new premises still have an edge. The expanded menu means even more difficult decisions at ordering time and the coffee remains excellent. Counter is still one of London's best destination cafés.

FOOD.

A delicious breakfast menu, baguettes, bagels, hearty homemade pies and cakes.

CONTACT.

+44(0)78 3427 5920
www.thecountercafe.co.uk
info@thecountercafe.co.uk
Hackney Wick

Sister coffee shops.
The Container Café

OVERVIEW.

Category
Artisanal Independent
Owner
Tom and Jess Seaton
Head barista
Will Collins
First opened
2009

COFFEE & EQUIPMENT.

Coffee roaster
Square Mile Coffee Roasters
Coffee machine
La Marzocco Linea, 2 groups
Coffee grinder
Anfim

COFFEE PRICING.

Espresso	£1.40
Cappuccino	£2.00
Latte	£2.50
Flat white	£2.00

RATING.

COFFEE 4.25 / 5

OVERALL 4.50 / 5

E5 Bakehouse

Arch 395, Mentmore Terrace, E8 3PH

OPEN.

Daily: 7:00am - 7:00pm

Tucked under the railway arches in London Fields, this busy bakery churns out hundreds of organic loaves of bread each day, as well as some seriously good coffee. With huge bags of flour stacked on the rough floorboards and the smell of baking bread filling the cavernous space, a visit to E5 Bakehouse is a truly warming and sensory experience - more like walking into an old-fashioned mill than an urban café. During the week, locals stop by for a chat, to read the papers or to grab their daily loaf, but on Saturdays, they queue out the door for fresh bagels. Baking classes are also popular.

FOOD.

A wide range of fresh breads, as well as pastries, sandwiches and soup.

CONTACT.

+44(0)75 4830 0244
www.e5bakehouse.com
info@e5bakehouse.com
Bethnal Green

OVERVIEW.

Category
Bakery Coffee Shop
Owner
Ben Mackinnon
Head barista
Asher Preston
First opened
2010

COFFEE & EQUIPMENT.

Coffee roaster
Nude Espresso
Coffee machine
Wega, 2 groups
Coffee grinder
Mazzer

COFFEE PRICING.

Espresso	£1.80
Cappuccino	£2.00
Latte	£2.00
Flat white	£2.00

RATING.

COFFEE 4.25 / 5

OVERALL 4.25 / 5

Esoteria

276 Hackney Road, E2 7SJ

OPEN.

Mon-Fri.	7:00am - 4:00pm
Sat-Sun.	9:30am - 5:00pm

Although it might look small from the outside, on the inside, Esoteria is full of surprises. Pies, cakes, pasta and a range of other fresh, delicious food awaits, along with bags of Nude Espresso, some cosy seating and an antique Bezzera Eagle coffee machine. Coffee is priced according to milk volume, giving customers complete control over the strength of their beverage, and locals flock here in the mornings for their takeaway espressos.

FOOD.

Homemade pies and sausage rolls, fresh sandwiches and savoury dishes, cakes, soups and salads, all made by chefs at The Marksman pub on the corner.

CONTACT.

+44(0)20 7739 7393

 Hoxton

Sister coffee shops.
The Marksman

OVERVIEW.

Category
Artisanal Independent

Owner
Gary Hedgecock

First opened
May 2011

COFFEE & EQUIPMENT.

Coffee roaster
Nude Espresso

Coffee machine
La Marzocco Linea, 3 groups

Coffee grinder
Mazzer

COFFEE PRICING.

Espresso	£1.50
Cappuccino	£2.00
Latte	£2.00 / £2.20
Flat white	£1.80

RATING.

COFFEE 4.25 / 5

OVERALL 4.00 / 5

Hackney

Fabrica

584 Kingsland Road, E8 4AH

OPEN.

Mon-Fri. 8:00am - 7:00pm
Sat. 9:00am - 7:00pm
Sun. 10:00am - 6:00pm

At first glance, Fabrica looks like many other coffee venues in London, but this excellent new venue has something special all of its very own. Owners Roberto and George are Italian and Greek respectively and their Mediterranean sensibilities combine to make Fabrica a stylish and satisfying destination that is a pleasant alternative to the usual laidback style of Kiwi and Aussie-owned cafés. The industrial interior furnished with mismatched tables and chairs gives way to a gorgeous outdoor area and, in a pleasing twist on the norm, coffee and tea arrive in glass cups and saucers, while water and juice are served in jars.

FOOD.

A menu of Italian-influenced breakfasts, lunches and snacks, with artisanal European deli foods also for sale.

CONTACT.

fabrica584@gmail.com
Dalston Junction

OVERVIEW.

Category
Artisanal Independent
Owner
Roberto Bassani and George Dellis
Head barista
George Dellis
First opened
October 2011

COFFEE & EQUIPMENT.

Coffee roaster
Monmouth Coffee Company
Coffee machine
Faema E61, 2 groups
Coffee grinder
Mazzer Jolly

COFFEE PRICING.

Espresso £1.40
Cappuccino £2.00
Latte £2.00
Flat white £2.00

RATING.

COFFEE
4.25 / 5

OVERALL
4.50 / 5

Fred & Fran

55 Kynaston Road, N16 0EB

OPEN.

Mon, Wed-Fri.	8:00am - 5:00pm
Tue.	Closed
Sat-Sun.	9:00am - 6:00pm

Tucked away on one of Stoke Newington's back streets is Fred & Fran, a warm and welcoming new café filled with the aroma of fresh baking. Owner Demelza Donohoo named Fred & Fran for her grandparents and applies the sort of care and attention to detail that was more typical of that generation to her exceptional venue. The beautiful Scandinavian-style interior is stylish and comfortable with blonde wood fittings and sleek, contemporary furniture and this look extends to the garden area. Every Square Mile coffee comes with a home-baked treat on the side.

FOOD.

A breakfast and lunch menu that includes quiches, soups and sandwiches and homemade cakes.

CONTACT.

+44(0)77 8815 8742
www.fredandfran.com
hello@fredandfran.com
Dalston Kingsland

OVERVIEW.

Category
Artisanal Independent
Owner
Demelza Donohoo
First opened
September 2011

COFFEE & EQUIPMENT.

Coffee roaster
Square Mile Coffee Roasters
Coffee machine
La Marzocco, 2 groups
Coffee grinder
Anfim

COFFEE PRICING.

Espresso	£1.40 / £1.90
Cappuccino	£2.20
Latte	£2.20
Flat white	£2.20

RATING.

COFFEE 4.25 / 5

OVERALL 4.25 / 5

Grind Coffee Bar Stratford

Lower ground floor, Westfield Stratford, E20 1EJ

A vast new shopping mall in the Olympic village is the last place you'd expect to find great coffee, but tucked away down one end of Westfield Stratford is the latest outpost of Putney café Grind. This new venue occupies a large, open-plan space that is designed to provide a respite from the bedlam of the shopping mall with large, kitchen-style tables, leather wingback chairs and a soothing New Zealand theme. Coffee is tailored for busy shoppers but more serious options are also available in the form of guest espressos, single-origin filters and home-brew kits.

FOOD.

A range of sweets and savouries all freshly baked on site each day.

CONTACT.

www.grindcoffeebar.co.uk
Stratford

Sister coffee shops.
Putney

OPEN.

Mon-Sat. 9:00am - 9:00pm
Sun. 11:00am - 6:00pm

Single-origin filter coffees and guest espressos are also available

OVERVIEW.

Category
Artisanal Independent
Owner
David and Tracey Dickinson
Head barista
Toby Glass
First opened
September 2011

COFFEE & EQUIPMENT.

Coffee roaster
London Coffee Roasters
Coffee machine
La Marzocco Strada 2 group and 3 group
Coffee grinder
Anfim Super Caimano x 3, Mazzer Super Jolly x 2

COFFEE PRICING.

Espresso	£1.50
Cappuccino	£2.20 / £2.70
Latte	£2.20 / £2.70
Flat white	£2.20 / £2.70

RATING.
COFFEE 4.25 / 5
OVERALL 4.25 / 5

The Hackney Pearl

11 Prince Edward Road, E9 5LX

OPEN.

Mon.	Closed
Tue-Sat.	10:00am - 11:00pm
Sun.	10:00am - 5:00pm

The Hackney Pearl is a stylish venue located in the middle of the vibrant Hackney Wick industrial area and is a favourite with the growing community of artists and urbanites. The broad glass shopfront allows in lots of natural light, and outdoor seating is also plentiful. The beautiful seasonal menu changes daily and an extensive bar list is available in case coffee isn't quite enough. Open until late every evening for dinner, drinks and events.

FOOD.

Paninis, soups, salads, cakes and a rotating a la carte menu.

CONTACT.

+44(0)20 8510 3605
www.thehackneypearl.com
info@thehackneypearl.com
Hackney Wick

OVERVIEW.

Category
Artisanal Independent
Owner
James Morgan
First opened
2009

COFFEE & EQUIPMENT.

Coffee roaster
Square Mile Coffee Roasters
Coffee machine
Gaggia D90, 3 groups
Coffee grinder
Mazzer Super Jolly

COFFEE PRICING.

Espresso	£1.70 / £2.10
Cappuccino	£2.00 / £2.40
Latte	£2.00 / £2.40
Flat white	£2.00 / £2.40

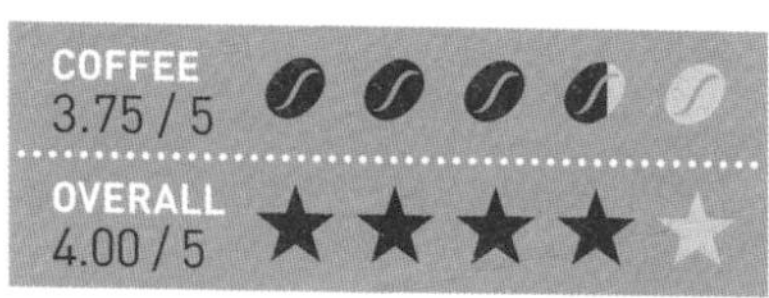

Hackney

Lemon Monkey

188 Stoke Newington High Street, N16 7JD

OPEN.

Mon-Sat. 9:00am - 6:00pm
Sun. 10:00am - 6:00pm

Open late some Fridays for events

Lemon Monkey is a cheerful, family-friendly Stoke Newington café and deli that is a favourite with the locals. Inside, Lemon Monkey is much larger than it appears from the street and, as well as plentiful seating, has shelves, tables and fridges stocked full of fresh produce, artisanal foods, chutneys and wine to take home. Mozzo coffee is served alongside a continental-style menu and the café stays open late some Friday evenings for events and live music.

FOOD.

An organic menu of breakfast options, salads, quiche, specialty cheeses and shared platters. A special children's menu.

CONTACT.

+44(0)20 7241 4454
www.lemon-monkey.co.uk
lemon.monkey@btconnect.com
Hackney Wick

OVERVIEW.

Category
Artisanal Independent

Owner
Katharine Tasker

First opened
2007

COFFEE & EQUIPMENT.

Coffee roaster
Mozzo

Coffee machine
La Marzocco Linea, 2 groups

Coffee grinder
Mazzer Luigi

COFFEE PRICING.

Espresso	£1.50 / £1.55
Cappuccino	£2.35 / £2.55
Latte	£2.35 / £2.55
Flat white	£2.30

RATING.

COFFEE 4.00 / 5

OVERALL 4.00 / 5

Mouse & De Lotz

103 Shacklewell Lane, E8 2EB

Hackney

OPEN.

Mon, Wed-Fri.	8:00am - 6:00pm
Tue.	Closed
Sat.	9:00am - 6:00pm
Sun.	10:00am - 6:00pm

To enter Mouse & De Lotz is to step back in time to an era of glass milk bottles, Singer sewing machines and cakes made by hand. Squashy sofas, window seats and a pretty, vintage aesthetic enhance the comforting retro feel, but free wifi brings this cafe right up to date and makes it an ideal place to spend a lazy hour. Superb coffee is prepared by a rotating staff of artists, students and parents, all of whom bring full-time passion to the food and drinks they prepare for their Dalston customers.

FOOD.

Hearty breakfast options, sandwiches and soups for lunch and a delectable range of homemade cakes baked daily.

CONTACT.

+44(0)20 3489 8082
www.mousedelotz.com
info@mousedelotz.com
Dalston Kingsland

OVERVIEW.

Category
Bakery Coffee Shop
Owner
Victoria Shard and Nadya Mousawi
Head barista
Tim Magalit
First opened
2010

COFFEE & EQUIPMENT.

Coffee roaster
Square Mile Coffee Roasters
Coffee machine
La Marzocco, 2 groups
Coffee grinder
Anfim

COFFEE PRICING.

Espresso	£1.80
Cappuccino	£2.20
Latte	£2.60
Flat white	£2.20

RATING.

COFFEE 4.25 / 5

OVERALL 4.25 / 5

Pacific Social Club

8 Clarence Road, E5 8HB

OPEN.

Mon-Fri. 7.30am - 7:00pm
Sat-Sun. 10:00am - 6:00pm

Need a tropical holiday but can't afford the airfare? Take a trip to Pacific Social Club, an oasis of retro Pacfic style in Lower Clapton. This relaxed café runs on island time and features diner bench seats, a crackly vinyl soundtrack, coffee in vintage cups and some of the best breakfast and brunch snacks in East London. Climpson's coffee is served alongside fresh juices, fruity cakes, and 1950s soft drinks in a two-room space decorated with old LP sleeves and tropical wallpaper.

FOOD.

A Pacific-influenced breakfast and lunch menu of toasts and sandwiches, plus fruit, locally sourced cakes and condiments, Nigerian soft drinks and candy.

CONTACT.

pacificsocialclub@gmail.com
Hackney Central

OVERVIEW.

Category
Artisanal Independent
Owner
Nick Goff and Liam Casey
Head barista
Nick Goff and Michael Giles
First opened
June 2011

COFFEE & EQUIPMENT.

Coffee roaster
Climpson & Sons
Coffee machine
La Marzocco Linea, 2 groups
Coffee grinder
Mazzer

COFFEE PRICING.

Espresso	£1.50 / £1.70
Cappuccino	£2.00 / £2.20
Latte	£2.00 / £2.20
Flat white	£2.20

RATING.

COFFEE 4.25 / 5

OVERALL 4.25 / 5

Pavilion

Corner Old Ford Rd & Grove Rd, Victoria Park, E9 7DE

OPEN.

Mon-Sun. 8:30am - 4:00pm

Perfectly positioned overlooking the lake, Pavilion offers excellent coffee and fresh food to the crowds of locals who flock to Victoria Park every day to walk their dogs, exercise, spend time with family or simply relax. The café itself features a striking domed glass roof and the outdoor balcony area offers stunning views over the lake and park. Pavilion's popular brunch menu is organic and locally sourced wherever possible and the British-style fare is best sampled on a sunny weekend, so arrive early to avoid the queue.

FOOD.

Cooked breakfasts, daily lunch menu, sandwiches, baked treats and cakes.

CONTACT.

+44(0)20 8980 0030
www.the-pavilion-cafe.com
Bethnal Green

Sister coffee shops.
Elliots (Redchurch Street)

OVERVIEW.

Category
Artisanal Independent
Owner
Brett Redman and Rob Green
First opened
2007

COFFEE & EQUIPMENT.

Coffee roaster
Square Mile Coffee Roasters
Coffee machine
Synesso Cyncra, 3 groups
Coffee grinder
Anfim

COFFEE PRICING.

Espresso	£1.50
Cappuccino	£2.20
Latte	£2.20
Flat white	£2.20

RATING.

COFFEE 4.00 / 5

OVERALL 4.00 / 5

Railroad

120-122 Morning Lane, E9 6LH

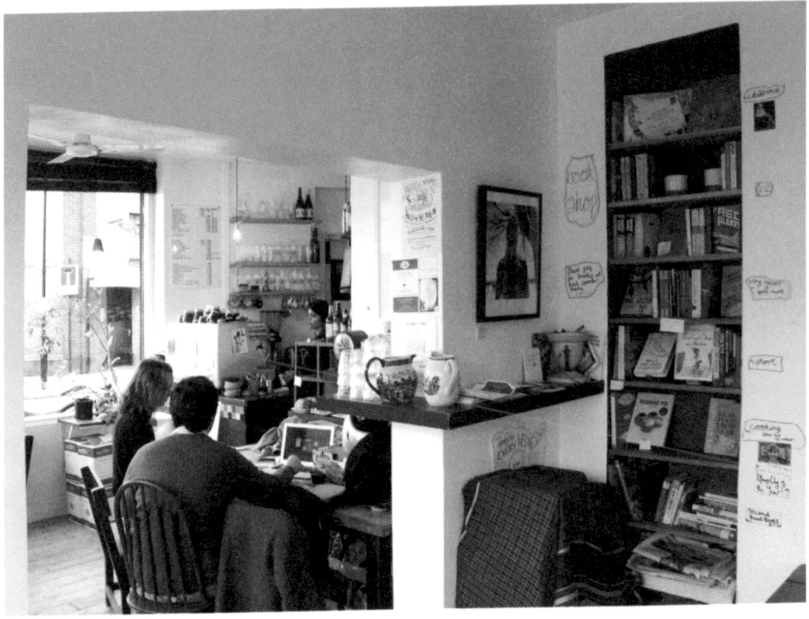

A visit to Railroad is food for both the body and the mind - the delicious and inventive seasonal menu (produced as if by magic from a tiny kitchen) is complemented by a small range of books for sale and a programme of regular musical and open-mic events. Square Mile coffee is served in handmade earthenware cups that lend themselves to being held in both hands on cold days and the café's sunny corner location makes it an ideal spot to sit and bask in the sunshine.

OPEN.

Sun-Tue. 10:00am - 5:00pm
Wed-Sat. 10:00am - 11:00pm

OVERVIEW.

Category
Eatery
Owner
Matt Doran and Liz Parle
First opened
2010

COFFEE & EQUIPMENT.

Coffee roaster
Square Mile Coffee Roasters
Coffee machine
Nuova Simonelli
Coffee grinder
Anfim

COFFEE PRICING.

Espresso	£1.50 / £1.90
Cappuccino	£2.20 / £2.40
Latte	£2.20 / £2.40
Flat white	£2.20 / £2.40

FOOD.

A small but constantly evolving menu of fresh, seasonal food, both for breakfast and dinner. Cakes and desserts also served.

CONTACT.

+44(0)20 8985 2858
www.railroadhackney.co.uk
Homerton

RATING.

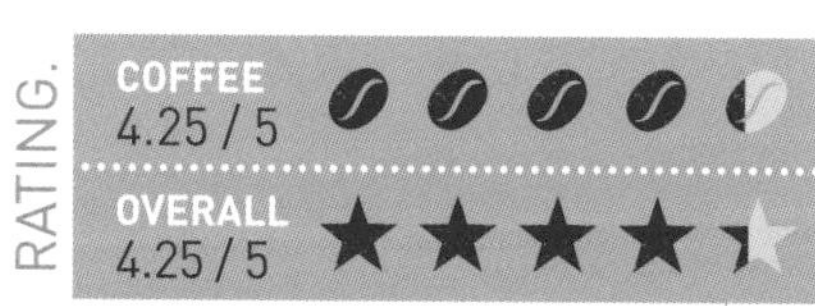

Reilly Rocket

507 Kingsland Road, E8 4AU

Situated behind a motorcycle shop on Kingsland Road, Reilly Rocket is the antidote to twee, chintzy cafés and industrial chic. Decorated with colourful memorabilia, cactus plants, brown leather sofas, taxidermy and graphic wall art, Reilly's is a haven for lovers of rebellion and retro road culture. Hunter S Thompson would have been right at home here and a memorial to British racing legend Barry Sheene adorns one wall. The coffee is just as gutsy and is pulled by a committed team of hardcore baristas.

OPEN.

Mon-Sat. 8:00am - 5:00pm
Sun. 9:00am - 4:00pm

OVERVIEW.

Category
Retail & Leisure
Owner
George Dennison
and Timothy Carmichael
Head barista
Clementine De Pressigny
First opened
April 2011

COFFEE & EQUIPMENT.

Coffee roaster
Square Mile Coffee Roasters
Coffee machine
La Marzocco Linea, 2 groups
Coffee grinder
Mazzer

COFFEE PRICING.

Espresso	£2.00
Cappuccino	£2.20
Latte	£2.40
Flat white	£2.20

FOOD.

A small, informal menu of breakfast and brunch snacks such as bagels and quesadillas, as well as cakes and muffins from a local supplier.

CONTACT.

Dalston Junction

RATING.

COFFEE
4.25 / 5

OVERALL
4.00 / 5

Hackney

Tina, We Salute You

TOP 30

47 King Henry's Walk, N1 4NH

OPEN.

Mon.	Closed
Tue-Fri.	8:00am - 7:00pm
Sat.	9:00am - 7:00pm
Sun.	10:00am - 7:00pm

Dalston locals are fiercely protective of Tina, We Salute You and the number of coffees chalked up on the clever loyalty wall proves just how much this café is loved. Every two months, the interior is given over to a local artist to use as an exhibition space and do with whatever they wish; this keeps things fresh and makes for a great talking point. The food is fresh and innovative and the coffee is among the best in town.

FOOD.

Choose from freshly made bagels, pastries, sandwiches and cakes, or something off the morning brunch menu.

CONTACT.

+44(0)20 3119 0047
www.tinawesaluteyou.com
tina@tinawesaluteyou.com
Dalston Kingsland

OVERVIEW.

Category
Artisanal Independent
Owner
Danny Hilton and Steve Hawkes
Head barista
Lou Hartman and Thomas Ward
First opened
2009

COFFEE & EQUIPMENT.

Coffee roaster
Square Mile Coffee Roasters
Coffee machine
La Marzocco Linea, 3 groups
Coffee grinder
Anfim, Mazzer

COFFEE PRICING.

Espresso	£1.50 / £1.80
Cappuccino	£2.40
Latte	£2.40
Flat white	£2.40

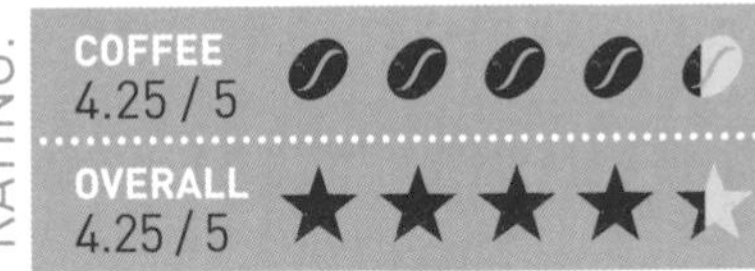

Towpath

42 De Beauvoir Crescent, N1 5SB

Hackney

Image supplied by Towpath

OPEN.

March 5 - November 5 only:

Tue-Fri. 8:00am - 5:00pm
Sat-Sun. 9:00am - 5:00pm

Tucked away alongside a bend of the canal in Hackney is Towpath, a relaxed, rustic venue that serves authentic Italian coffee and a selection of homemade meals and snacks. Alfresco tables provide fantastic spots to watch passersby on the canalside pavement and a communal table adds to the neighbourly feel of this hidden gem. Be sure to try an affogato - Towpath makes its own soft-serve ice cream.

FOOD.

Choose from breakfast, quiche, savoury tarts, cakes and daily specials.

CONTACT.

+44(0)20 7254 7606

Dalston Kingsland

No takeaway coffees, unless with own cup

OVERVIEW.

Category
Artisanal Independent
Owner
Jason Lowe and Lori de Mori
Head barista
Amanda Thompson
First opened
2010

COFFEE & EQUIPMENT.

Coffee roaster
Piansa
Coffee machine
La Marzocco Linea manual, 2 groups
Coffee grinder
Eureka Conti Valerio

COFFEE PRICING.

Espresso	£1.50
Cappuccino	£2.20
Latte	£2.20

RATING.

COFFEE 3.75 / 5

OVERALL 3.75 / 5

Wilton Way Café

63 Wilton Way, E8 1BG

One of the first and best venues in a wave of new Hackney café openings in recent years, Wilton Way Café combines superb coffee and fresh, simple food with art and music to create an outstanding coffee experience. Incorporating clever modular furniture, rotating art exhibits, a busy coffee bar, a generous display of cakes and a radio corner for live local broadcasts, Wilton's makes excellent use of its intimate but vibrant space and generates something special in terms of a buzzing, creative atmosphere. Visit on a sunny Saturday to enjoy a fine cup of coffee on the footpath outside along with the crowds of faithful Wilton's acolytes.

OPEN.

Mon-Fri.	8:00am - 5:00pm
Sat.	8:00am - 6:00pm
Sun.	9:00am - 6:00pm

OVERVIEW.

Category
Artisanal Independent
Owner
David McHugh
Head barista
Claire Madiot and Josie Beevers
First opened
2009

COFFEE & EQUIPMENT.

Coffee roaster
Climpson & Sons
Coffee machine
La Marzocco Linea, 2 groups
Coffee grinder
Mazzer Super Jolly

COFFEE PRICING.

Espresso	£1.50 / £1.70
Cappuccino	£2.20 / £2.40
Latte	£2.20 / £2.40
Flat white	£2.20 / £2.40

FOOD.

The all-day breakfast and lunch menu includes sourdough toasts, bacon baps and sandwiches.

CONTACT.

+44(0)20 7249 0444
www.londonfieldsradio.com
dom@londonfieldsradio.com
Hackney Central

RATING.

COFFEE 4.50 / 5

OVERALL 4.50 / 5

South East London

London's thriving South East is home to some exciting newcomers on the coffee scene this year, particularly boutique roasteries. Along with its vibrant fine food market scene, this area of the city is rapidly establishing itself on the coffee map.

Browns of Brockley

5 Coulgate Street, SE4 2RW

A stylish café and deli opposite the Brockley train station, Browns has rapidly developed a reputation as one of the only places to go for a good coffee in the area. With its simple layout and natural colour scheme, Browns is a cosy and relaxing place to step in and slow down. Bookshelves house record collections, books to peruse and the odd board game to play with fellow caffeine hunters at the communal table. Beautiful photography decorating the walls is for sale.

OPEN.

Mon-Wed.	7:00am - 7:00pm
Thu.	7:00am - 11:00pm
Fri.	7:00am - 7:00pm
Sat.	9:00am - 5:00pm
Sun.	9:00am - 4:00pm

OVERVIEW.

Category
Artisanal Independent
Owner
Ross Brown
Head barista
Will Riley
First opened
2009

COFFEE & EQUIPMENT.

Coffee roaster
Square Mile Coffee Roasters
Coffee machine
La Marzocco Linea, 2 groups
Coffee grinder
Mazzer Robur E

COFFEE PRICING.

Espresso	£1.50
Cappuccino	£2.50
Latte	£2.50
Flat white	£2.50

FOOD.

A selection of fresh deli-style foods including croissants, pastries, cakes and sandwiches.

CONTACT.

+44(0)20 8692 0722
ross@brownsofbrockley.com
Brockley

RATING.

COFFEE
4.50 / 5

OVERALL
4.50 / 5

The Deptford Project

121-123 Deptford High Street, SE8 4NS

The Deptford Project is an innovative café and bistro in the shell of a decommissioned 1960s train carriage that has occupied a site on Deptford High Street since 2008. Now a local fixture, the Project remains a delightfully quirky community hub, particularly on Deptford Market days - Wednesday, Friday and Saturday - when it attracts a constant stream of local artists and residents. Colourful, frequently changing street art covers the exterior of the café and the outside decking provides the perfect spot to soak up some sunshine on warm days.

OPEN.

Mon-Sat. 9:00am - 6:00pm
Sun. 9:00am - 5:00pm

OVERVIEW.

Category
Artisanal Independent
Owner
Rebecca Molina
First opened
2008

COFFEE & EQUIPMENT.

Coffee roaster
Darlington's
Coffee machine
La Marzocco, 2 groups
Coffee grinder
Espresso Italiano

COFFEE PRICING.

Espresso	£1.40 / £1.70
Cappuccino	£2.20
Latte	£2.20
Flat white	£2.10

FOOD.

Fresh organic quiches, salads and baked potatoes are prepared on site.

CONTACT.

+44(0)75 4559 3279
www.thedeptfordproject.com
rebecca@thedeptfordproject.com
Deptford Bridge

RATING.

Monmouth Coffee Company

2 Park Street, SE1 9AB

Monmouth Coffee Company has developed a cult-like following among many Londoners who make weekly pilgrimages to their coffee mecca. The Borough Market site, larger than Monmouth's Covent Garden premises, is incredibly popular with market regulars and tourists and is appropriately surrounded by some of the city's finest producers of foods and beverages. Fridays and Saturdays are extremely busy, so to fully immerse yourself in the Monmouth experience, a weekday visit is a safer bet. Also worth a visit is Monmouth's roastery, just a short journey away at 34 Maltby Street in Bermondsey, which is open for a few hours on Saturdays only.

The Borough

OPEN.

Mon-Sat. 7:30am - 6:00pm
Sun. Closed

OVERVIEW.

Category
Artisanal Independent
Owner
Anita Le Roy
First opened
2001

COFFEE & EQUIPMENT.

Coffee roaster
Monmouth Coffee Company
Coffee machine
La Marzocco Linea,
2 groups x 2
Coffee grinder
Mazzer Robur E, Mazzer Robur

Sister coffee shops.
Covent Garden /
Bermondsey (Roastery)

Also serves **single-origin filter coffee.** Monmouth Coffee Company roastery located nearby in Bermondsey

COFFEE PRICING.

Espresso	£1.35
Cappuccino	£2.35
Latte	£2.35
Flat white	£2.35

FOOD.

Help yourself to bread and jam on the communal tables, or try a croissant or brioche from the counter.

CONTACT.

+44(0)20 7232 3010
www.monmouthcoffee.co.uk
beans@monmouthcoffee.co.uk
London Bridge

RATING.

COFFEE 4.75 / 5
OVERALL 4.50 / 5

ScooterCaffè

132 Lower Marsh, SE1 7AE

OPEN.

Mon-Thu.	8:30am - 11:00pm
Fri.	8:30am - 12:00am
Sat.	10:00am - 12:00am
Sun.	12:00pm - 10:00pm

The brainchild of ex-aircraft engineer Craig O'Dwyer, ScooterCaffè started life as a Vespa workshop. O'Dwyer soon branched out into coffee and now his collection of vintage machinery and scooter memorabilia adorns a unique café space. Events are held in the basement, while a sunny courtyard out the back provides space for contemplation. Coffee is made on a 1957 Faema espresso machine and a bring-your-own food policy means the menu is up to you. ScooterCaffè is one of London's most unique retro experiences and a must-visit for those who like their coffee with some va-va-voom.

FOOD.

Bring-your-own food policy.
Some sweets and snacks available.

CONTACT.

+44(0)20 7620 1421
scootercaffe@googlemail.com
Lambeth North

Sister coffee shops.
Cable Café

OVERVIEW.

Category
Artisanal Independent
Owner / Head barista
Craig O'Dwyer
First opened
2009

COFFEE & EQUIPMENT.

Coffee roaster
Londinium
Coffee machine
1957 Faema, 3 groups
Coffee grinder
Quick Mill, vintage Omer

COFFEE PRICING.

Espresso	£1.50 / £2.00
Cappuccino	£2.10
Latte	£2.10
Flat white	£2.10

RATING.

COFFEE 4.25 / 5

OVERALL 4.25 / 5

St. David Coffee House

5 David's Road, SE23 3EP

OPEN.

Mon.	Closed
Tue-Fri.	8:00am - 6:00pm
Sat.	9:00am - 5:00pm
Sun.	10:00am - 3:30pm

St. David Coffee House is a truly unique café, a London oddity that is firmly rooted in its community. Local artists, actors, musicians and families come here in droves to sip espresso among the books, stacks of vinyl, vintage movie memorabilia and old 8-tracks, and enjoy the local art displays and free wifi. Coffee is served in vintage cups and the charming Edwardian frontage admits plenty of natural light.

FOOD.

Locally supplied cakes, pastries and sandwiches, salads, soups.

CONTACT.

+44(0)20 8291 6646
www.stdavidcoffeehouse.co.uk
info@stdavidcoffeehouse.co.uk
Forest Hill

OVERVIEW.

Category
Artisanal Independent
Owner
Dan Shardlow and Lisa Etherington
Head barista
Dan Shardlow and Jimmy Metherell
First opened
2010

COFFEE & EQUIPMENT.

Coffee roaster
Square Mile Coffee Roasters
Coffee machine
Rancilio Classe 10
Coffee grinder
Anfim

COFFEE PRICING.

Espresso	£1.40 / £1.60
Cappuccino	1.80 / £2.00
Latte	£2.00
Flat white	£1.90

RATING.

COFFEE 4.00 / 5

OVERALL 4.00 / 5

South East London

Taylor St Baristas Canary Wharf

8 South Colonnade, E14 4PZ

The coffee-lovers of Canary Wharf are rejoicing at the arrival of Taylor St Baristas' new venue on South Colonnade. This lean, mean café is designed to produce a high volume of quality coffee for the district's bankers and business people and uses two 3-group Nuova Simonelli Aurelias (for takeaway coffees), one 2-group Synesso (for guest espresso only) and six grinders to do this, as well as a range of other specialty brewing equipment. A full breakfast and brunch menu is also on offer and Australian Freddo chocolate frogs and Caramel Koalas offer a touch of sunshine on grey London days.

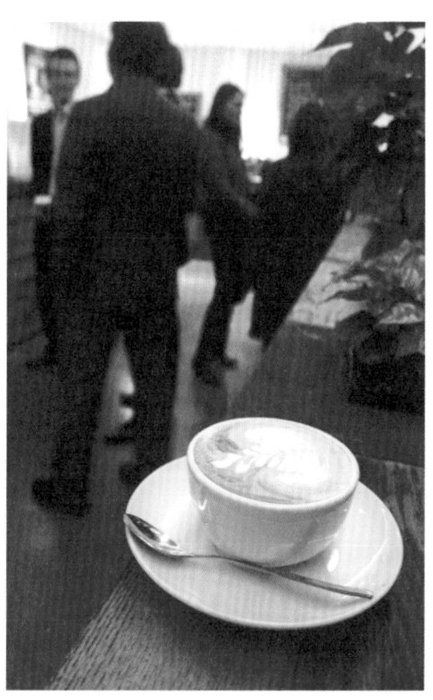

COFFEE PRICING.

Espresso	£1.60
Cappuccino	£2.40 / £2.70
Latte	£2.70
Flat white	£2.40 / £3.00

FOOD.

A generous breakfast and lunch menu, cakes, lamingtons and Australian candy.

CONTACT.

+44(0)774 8805 106
www.taylor-st.com
Canary Wharf

OPEN.

Mon-Fri.	7:00am - 5:00pm
Sat-Sun.	Closed

OVERVIEW.

Category
Chain
Owner
Nick, Andrew and Laura Tolley
Head barista
Dennis Tutbury
First opened
December 2011

COFFEE & EQUIPMENT.

Coffee roaster
Union Hand-Roasted, Has Bean, Square Mile and others
Coffee machine
2 x Nuova Simonelli Aurelia, 3 groups and 1 x Synesso Cyncra, 2 groups
Coffee grinder
2 x Mazzer Robur E, 2 x Mazzer Major E, 2 x Anfim Super Caimano, Mahlkönig Tanzania

Sister coffee shops.
Six other locations in London and Brighton

RATING.
COFFEE 4.50 / 5
OVERALL 4.25 / 5

South West London

South West London contains a dizzying array of cultural influences, from the Afro-Caribbean heritage of Brixton to the antipodean-influenced lifestyle of Clapham and the genteel suburban rhythms of Putney. The area's colourful and creative coffee culture reflects these unique influences and local quirks.

Artisan

203 Upper Richmond Road, SW15 6SG

OPEN.

Mon-Fri. 7:30am - 6:30pm
Sat-Sun. 8:30am - 5:30pm

"Obsessively passionate about coffee" is the motto at Artisan and this sums up the philosophy of this charming new café in Putney. Artisan's warm, light-filled space is imbued with the aroma of freshly ground Allpress coffee and furnished with quirky designer furniture. Fine artisan foods from local suppliers are displayed on the corrugated iron counter and happy local mums take advantage of the plentiful seating, friendly welcome and pram space. Particularly inventive is Artisan's diverting loyalty scheme, which allows customers to spin a wheel to determine their reward.

FOOD.

Breakfast granola, soups, sandwiches and cakes from a local supplier.

CONTACT.

www.artisancoffee.co.uk
info@artisancoffee.co.uk
East Putney

OVERVIEW.

Category
Artisanal Independent
Owner
Edwin Harrison and Magda Woloszy
First opened
November 2011

COFFEE & EQUIPMENT.

Coffee roaster
Allpress
Coffee machine
La Marzocco FB/80, 2 groups
Coffee grinder
La Marzocco

COFFEE PRICING.

Espresso	£1.50
Cappuccino	£2.20
Latte	£2.20
Flat white	£2.20

RATING.

COFFEE 4.25 / 5

OVERALL 4.00 / 5

Barossa

277 New Kings Road, SW6 4RD

OPEN.

Mon-Fri.	8:00am - 5:00pm
Sat.	9:00am - 5:00pm
Sun.	9:00am - 4:00pm

Barossa, formerly known as Di'Zain, is a stylish café in an area otherwise lacking quality coffee shops. Barossa's interior is modern and sophisticated, staff are friendly and the brunch menu offers something to suit all tastes. Barossa is also open as an Australian-style wine and tapas bar during the evening, and a recent switch to Caravan coffee indicates a new commitment to providing seriously excellent coffee.

FOOD.

Australian-style breakfast and brunch, tapas menu in the evenings.

CONTACT.

+44(0)20 7751 9711
www.thebarossa.co.uk
info@thebarossa.co.uk
Parsons Green

OVERVIEW.

Category
Artisanal Independent
Owner
Emily Cook and Katie Newton Darby
Head barista
Mike Logue
First opened
2009

COFFEE & EQUIPMENT.

Coffee roaster
Caravan
Coffee machine
La Marzocco Linea, 2 groups
Coffee grinder
Mazzer Robur E

COFFEE PRICING.

Espresso	£1.80
Cappuccino	£2.50
Latte	£2.60
Flat white	£2.50

RATING.

COFFEE 4.00 / 5

OVERALL 4.00 / 5

Birdhouse

123 St. John's Hill, SW11 1SZ

This perfectly formed cafe and eatery is an exciting new addition to Battersea's St. John's Hill. Coffee is carefully prepared and served in an interior that is light, beautifully furnished in brushed steel, grey felt and vintage wood, and punctuated with splashes of bright yellow. Imagery of birds adorns the walls and yellow mesh baskets complete the avian feel. Delicious fresh sandwiches, cookies and cakes are arrayed on an old carpenter's block, and food is served in tin trays. Takeaway customers will love the coded stamps that decorate coffee cups (feather = flat white).

OPEN.

Mon-Fri. 7:00am - 4:00pm
Sat-Sun. 9:00am - 5:00pm

OVERVIEW.

Category
Artisanal Independent
Owner
Cameron Rosen
Head barista
Alexei Morales
First opened
October 2011

COFFEE & EQUIPMENT.

Coffee roaster
Climpson & Sons
Coffee machine
La Marzocco Linea, 3 groups
Coffee grinder
Anfim

COFFEE PRICING.

Espresso	£1.80
Cappuccino	£2.20
Latte	£2.20
Flat white	£2.20

FOOD.

Gourmet sandwiches containing ingredients such as Serrano ham, candied walnuts and roast tomatoes. Fresh cakes, cookies and friands baked on site.

CONTACT.

+44(0)20 7228 6663
www.birdhou.se
Clapham Junction

RATING.
COFFEE 4.50 / 5
OVERALL 4.25 / 5

TOP 30

The Black Lab Coffee House

18 Clapham Common Southside, SW4 7AB

OPEN.

Mon-Fri. 8:00am - 5:00pm
Sat. 9:00am - 5:00pm
Sun. 10:00am - 5:00pm

The Black Lab Coffee House is a warm and cosy choice in an area surprisingly light on good cafés. This venue combines Italian influences (a traditional Gaggia machine and Italian-style coffee bar) with a local roast by Climpson & Sons to create coffee that is rooted in the past but in touch with modern tastes. As well as excellent coffee, the Black Lab serves a range of pastries and cakes sourced from a local patisserie and this is a great spot to spend a Sunday morning reading the papers over a cappuccino, or to grab a takeaway coffee on the way to nearby Clapham Common.

FOOD.

Filled ciabbatas, focaccias, toasted paninis and a tempting choice of tarts, cakes and cookies.

CONTACT.

+44(0)20 7738 8441
www.blacklabcoffee.com
info@blacklabcoffee.com
Clapham Common

OVERVIEW.

Category
Artisanal Independent
Owner
James and Matthew Goodman
Head barista
Matthew Goodman and Alessandro Castellani
First opened
2010

COFFEE & EQUIPMENT.

Coffee roaster
Climpson & Sons
Coffee machine
Gaggia D90, 2 groups
Coffee grinder
Mahlkönig K30

COFFEE PRICING.

Espresso	£1.80
Cappuccino	£2.40
Latte	£2.40
Flat white	£2.40

RATING.
COFFEE 4.25 / 5
OVERALL 4.25 / 5

Brew

45 Northcote Road, SW11 1NJ

OPEN.

Mon-Sat. 7:00am - 10:00pm
Sun. 7:30am - 6:00pm

A favourite with the Northcote Road set, Brew is a cheerful antidote to the many chain coffee stores nearby. Simple and cosy, Brew offers Union coffee and a comprehensive menu in a breezy, laidback environment. However, this café is best known for its sensational breakfasts, which feature only the best-quality local ingredients, as well as juices and smoothies. A tantalising new dinner menu is now on offer and is complemented by a beer and wine list.

FOOD.

Antipodean-style menu including poached eggs, salads, toasted pides and muffins, and a new selection of dishes for dinner.

CONTACT.

+44(0)20 7585 2198
www.brew-cafe.com
brewnorthcote@gmail.com
Clapham Junction

OVERVIEW.

Category
Artisanal Independent
Owner
Jason Wells
Head barista
Leann St. Clair
First opened
2008

COFFEE & EQUIPMENT.

Coffee roaster
Union Hand-Roasted
Coffee machine
La Marzocco Linea, 2 groups
Coffee grinder
Mazzer Luigi srl

COFFEE PRICING.

Espresso	£2.00 / £2.20
Cappuccino	£2.50
Latte	£2.50
Flat white	£2.50

RATING.

COFFEE 4.25 / 5

OVERALL 4.00 / 5

Federation Coffee

Unit 77-78 Brixton Village Market, Coldharbour Lane, SW9 8PS ....

OPEN.

Mon-Fri.	8:00am - 5:00pm
Sat.	9:30am - 5:00pm
Sun.	Closed

Since opening in the redeveloped Brixton Village Market in early 2010, Federation Coffee has led a flowering of foodie culture in Brixton. Having moved to a larger site within the market due to its booming popularity, Federation is now surrounded by a host of other cafés and eateries that have followed its lead, and second outlet for its excellent coffee has also opened at Piano House on Brighton Terrace. With plans to roast its own coffee, Federation is one of the most exciting names in coffee south of the Thames.

FOOD.

A selection of homemade cakes, muffins and biscuits.

CONTACT.

www.federationcoffee.com
info@federationcoffee.com
 Brixton

OVERVIEW.

Category
Artisanal Independent
Owner / Head barista
George Wallace and Nick Coates
First opened
2010

COFFEE & EQUIPMENT.

Coffee roaster
Federation and Nude Espresso
Coffee machine
La Marzocco Linea, 3 groups
Coffee grinder
Mazzer

COFFEE PRICING.

Espresso	£1.50
Cappuccino	£2.20
Latte	£2.20
Flat white	£2.20

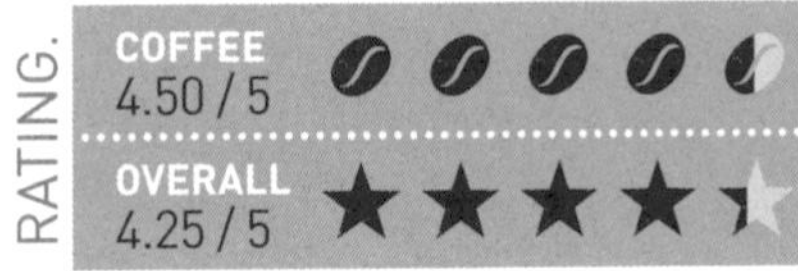

Grind Coffee Bar Putney

79 Lower Richmond Road, SW15 1ET

OPEN.

Mon-Fri. 7:00am - 5:00pm
Sat-Sun. 8:30am - 5:00pm

This stylish, contemporary café was one of the pioneers on the now-thriving Putney coffee scene upon opening in 2010 and has become a firm local favourite. Grind's friendly Antipodean atmosphere and excellent flat whites make it popular with local ex-pats, but its bespoke house blend from London Coffee Roasters and use of British ingredients gives it a decidedly local outlook. The café's corner location and tempting range of homemade cakes, biscuits and savouries make it difficult to pass without popping in for a coffee and a chat with a genial team of baristas.

FOOD.

Filled gourmet focaccias and ciabattas, scones, muffins, NZ-style cakes and biscuits made daily on site.

CONTACT.

+44(0)20 8789 5101
www.grindcoffeebar.co.uk
admin@grindcoffeebar.co.uk
Putney Bridge

Sister coffee shops.
Westfield Stratford

OVERVIEW.

Category
Artisanal Independent
Owner
David and Tracey Dickinson
Head barista
David Dickinson
First opened
2010

COFFEE & EQUIPMENT.

Coffee roaster
London Coffee Roasters
Coffee machine
La Marzocco Strada MP, 3 groups
Coffee grinder
Anfim Super Caimano x 2

COFFEE PRICING.

Espresso	£1.50 / £2.00
Cappuccino	£2.00 / £2.60
Latte	£2.00 / £2.60
Flat white	£2.00 / £2.60

RATING.

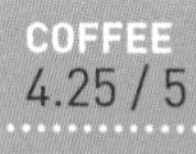

COFFEE 4.25 / 5

OVERALL 4.00 / 5

Le Pain Quotidien Parsons Green

70 Parsons Green Lane, SW6 4HU

OPEN.

Mon-Fri.	7:00am - 10:00pm
Sat.	8:00am - 10:00pm
Sun.	8:00am - 7:00pm

Le Pain Quotidien is an airy and welcoming boulangerie and café on Parsons Green Lane. Booth seats in recycled horse stables are a charming feature, along with the signature Le Pain Quotidien communal table highlighted with pretty drop lights. The atmosphere inside is refined and peaceful, with classical music, high ceilings and exposed brick walls. Enjoy a coffee while you linger over breakfast.

FOOD.

Organic sourdough breads and pastries made fresh on site daily. An all-day menu of tartines, salads, hot dishes and sweet snacks.

CONTACT.

+44(0)20 7486 6154
www.lepainquotidien.co.uk
parsonsgreen@lpquk.biz
Parsons Green

Sister coffee shops.
17 other stores in London

OVERVIEW.

Category
Bakery Coffee Shop
Owner
Le Pain Quotidien
First opened
2009

Filter coffee is also available

COFFEE & EQUIPMENT.

Coffee roaster
Miko Puro
Coffee machine
Faema Emblema, 2 groups
Coffee grinder
Mazzer Luigi srl x 2

COFFEE PRICING.

Espresso	£1.45 / £1.80
Cappuccino	£2.20 / £2.50
Latte	£2.20 / £2.50

RATING.

COFFEE 3.50 / 5

OVERALL 3.75 / 5

The Roastery (Bullet Coffee Cartel)

789 Wandsworth Road, SW8 3JQ

OPEN.

Mon-Wed. 7:30am - 3:30pm
Thu-Fri. 7:30am - 4:30pm
Sat-Sun. 9:00am - 4:30pm

Located on the sunny side of busy Wandsworth Road, The Roastery does everything it says on the tin, and more. As well as roasting its own beans and supplying them to venues around London, the café serves delicious food and coffee to enthusiastic Wandsworth regulars. The retro 1960s-style decor of the cafe contrasts with the industrial edge of the Toper roaster out back and customers can venture out of their seats to watch the roasting process from beginning to end.

FOOD.

A brunch menu, homemade cakes, biscuits and snacks.

CONTACT.

+44(0)20 7350 1961
www.bullet-coffee.com
info@bullet-coffee.com
Clapham Common

OVERVIEW.

Category
Artisanal Independent
Owner
Phil Ross
Head barista
Krystle Goodin
First opened
2009

COFFEE & EQUIPMENT.

Coffee roaster
Bullet Coffee Cartel
Coffee machine
Modified/PID La Marzocco Linea, 3 groups
Coffee grinder
Mazzer x 3

COFFEE PRICING.

Espresso	£1.50
Cappuccino	£2.40
Latte	£2.40
Flat white	£2.40

RATING.

COFFEE 4.25 / 5

OVERALL 4.00 / 5

West London

The neighbourhoods of West London have a village feel and the coffee scene is geared towards those who enjoy the finer things in life. Well-heeled locals mix with curious tourists in the area's upmarket restaurants, local cafés and fashion boutiques.

Ca'puccino

138a King's Road, SW3 4XB

OPEN.

Daily: 8:00am - 8:30pm

Bringing the Italian coffee experience to London, Ca'puccino offers a modern take on Italy's traditional coffee-bar culture. Across two levels, customers can enjoy coffee standing at a high table or relax in spacious white leather chairs. The Italian-inspired atmosphere is laidback and provides an agreeable setting for a lazy afternoon enjoying coffee with friends. A selection of freshly made ice cream, imported Italian desserts and savoury fare is also on offer.

FOOD.

Italian pastries, gelato and savoury fare.

CONTACT.

+44(0)20 7036 0555
www.ca-puccino.com
info@ca-puccino.com
Sloane Square

Sister coffee shops.
Westfield London / Harrods

OVERVIEW.

Category
Bakery Coffee Shop
Owner
Giacomo Moncalvo
Head barista
Ali Kollcaku
First opened
2011

COFFEE & EQUIPMENT.

Coffee roaster
Italian house blend
Coffee machine
La Cimbali

COFFEE PRICING.

Espresso	£1.50 / £2.00
Cappuccino	£2.10 / £2.80
Latte	£2.10 / £2.80
Flat white	£2.10

RATING.

COFFEE 4.00 / 5

OVERALL 4.00 / 5

Coffee Plant

180 Portobello Road, W11 2EB

OPEN.

Mon-Sat.	7:45am - 5:15pm
Sun.	9:00am - 4:30pm

Coffee Plant is a popular, grungy coffee hangout on Notting Hill's bustling Portobello Road. The café began life as a roastery, which can now be found in Acton. Coffee Plant supplies not only this shop but several others around London and staff here will also grind coffee beans to order. The clientele ranges from young backpackers to business people and everyone in between.

FOOD.

A selection of basic sandwiches and pastries, organic confectionery and chocolate.

CONTACT.

+44(0)20 7221 8137
www.coffee.uk.com
Ladbroke Grove

OVERVIEW.

Category
Artisanal Independent
Owner
Ian Henshall
First opened
2000

COFFEE & EQUIPMENT.

Coffee roaster
Coffee Plant
Coffee machine
Iberital Ladri, 2 groups x 2
Coffee grinder
Macap

COFFEE PRICING.

Espresso	£1.30
Cappuccino	£2.00
Latte	£2.00
Flat white	£2.00

RATING.

Gail's Queen's Park

75 Salusbury Road, NW6 6NH

OPEN.

Mon-Fri.	7:00am - 8:00pm
Sat.	8:00am - 8:00pm
Sun.	8:00am - 7:00pm

This Gail's venue created considerable buzz in the Queen's Park neighbourhood when it opened and has since become a favourite with the local residents. The signature display of appetising sandwiches, cakes and baked treats is on show out front, while a cosy seating area to the rear provides a quiet spot to relax and enjoy a Union coffee. This modern space is a great place to escape for a long lunch or afternoon tea with friends.

FOOD.

A fresh and colourful range of sandwiches, salads, pastries and cakes made on site.

CONTACT.

+44(0)20 7625 0068
www.gailsbread.co.uk
qp@gailsbread.co.uk
Queen's Park

Sister coffee shops.
Hampstead / Notting Hill / St. Johns Wood / Battersea / Chiswick

OVERVIEW.

Category
Chain
Owner
Ran Avidan and Tom Molnar
Head barista
Zuzana Lutwerdva
First opened
2010

COFFEE & EQUIPMENT.

Coffee roaster
Union Hand-Roasted
Coffee machine
La Marzocco Linea, 3 groups
Coffee grinder
Mazzer Super Jolly

COFFEE PRICING.

Espresso	£2.00 / £2.30
Cappuccino	£2.70 / £2.95
Latte	£2.70 / £2.95
Flat white	£2.70 / £2.95

RATING.

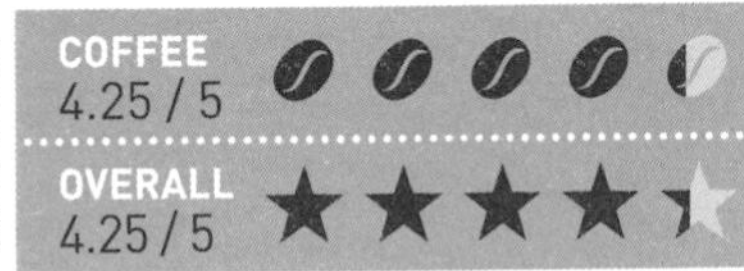

Ladurée Harrods

87/135 Brompton Road, SW1X 7XL

OPEN.

Mon-Sat.	9:00am - 9:00pm
Sun.	11:30am - 6:00pm

Located within the chic surroundings of Harrods, Ladurée is a visual and gastronomic delight. Immaculately presented sweets and treats are on offer, including the French patisserie's famous selection of pastel-coloured macarons. Customers can enjoy coffee and cake seated within the opulent marble interior or, on a sunny day, at an outdoor table.

FOOD.

Ladurée is famous for its macarons and French patisserie; a savoury menu is also on offer.

CONTACT.

+44(0)20 3155 0111
www.laduree.fr
ladureeharrods@laduree.com
Knightsbridge

Sister coffee shops.
38 stores globally

OVERVIEW.

Category
Grand Traditional
Owner
David Holder
Head barista
Benedict MacDonald
First opened
2005

COFFEE & EQUIPMENT.

Coffee roaster
Lavazza
Coffee machine
WMF
Coffee grinder
WMF

COFFEE PRICING.

Espresso	£2.30
Cappuccino	£3.25
Latte	£3.25
Flat white	£3.25

RATING.

COFFEE 3.50 / 5

OVERALL 4.25 / 5

Tomtom Coffee House

114 Ebury Street, SW1W 9QD

OPEN.

Mon-Fri. 8:00am - 9:00pm
Sat-Sun. 9:00am - 9:00pm

A Belgravia favourite, Tomtom Coffee House has a neighbourhood vibe with an upmarket feel. A large round table and an abundance of natural light fosters a friendly and communal atmosphere, making this a lovely choice for a lazy afternoon coffee with friends. Tomtom roasts its own coffee as well as several other house blends that are available for customers to purchase. Sister shop, Tomtom Cigars, is conveniently located across the road on Elizabeth Street.

FOOD.

All-day breakfast, Tomtom toasties, salads, soups, dips, platters and baked goods.

CONTACT.

+44(0)20 7730 1771
www.tomtom.co.uk
coffee@tomtom.co.uk
Sloane Square

OVERVIEW.

Category
Artisanal Independent
Owner
Tom Assheton
Head barista
Irina Timoshenko and Gena Kasatkins
First opened
2008

COFFEE & EQUIPMENT.

Coffee roaster
Tomtom (Charles Reid)
Coffee machine
La Marzocco Linea, 2 groups
Coffee grinder
Mazzer

COFFEE PRICING.

Espresso	£1.80
Cappuccino	£2.60
Latte	£2.60
Flat white	£2.90

RATING.

COFFEE 4.00 / 5

OVERALL 3.75 / 5

Coffee Glossary

Acidity: one of the principal categories used by professional tasters to determine the quality of a coffee or blend along with flavour, aroma and body. Usually refers to the pleasant tartness of a fine coffee and not the pH level.

AeroPress: a hand-powered device for brewing coffee that forces water through ground coffee at high pressure.

Affogato: a coffee-based dessert - usually a scoop of vanilla ice cream topped with a shot of hot espresso.

Americano, Caffè Americano: an espresso with hot water added.

Arabica, Coffea arabica: the earliest cultivated species of coffee tree and still the most widely grown. Arabica produces approximately 70% of the world's coffee and is dramatically superior in cup quality to other principal commercial coffee species such as Coffea canephora or Robusta.

Aroma: the way a coffee smells. Aroma is one of the principal categories used by professional tasters to determine the quality of a particular coffee or blend. Examples of aromas include earthy, spicy, floral and nutty.

Blend: a combination of coffees from different countries and regions that achieve a taste no single coffee can offer alone.

Body: the heaviness, thickness or relative weight of coffee on the tongue when tasted. Body is one of the principal categories used by professional tasters to determine the quality of a coffee or blend.

Brew group: in an espresso machine, the brew group contains the portafilter and group head. It needs to be heated in order to brew espresso.

Brew temperature: is dependent on the extraction method. For filter and French press, water should be just below boiling, and the consensus is that espresso should be brewed with water at 88-120°C.

Brew time: the time it takes for an espresso to pour from a portafilter spout - one of the key indicators of a good espresso shot. The guideline for an espresso brew time is 25-30 seconds.

Café au lait: one-third drip coffee with two-thirds hot frothed milk.

Café con leche: a traditional Spanish coffee consisting of espresso served with scalded milk.

Café mocha or mocha: similar to a caffè latte, but with added chocolate syrup or powder.

Caffeine: an odourless, bitter alkaloid responsible for the stimulating effect of coffee and tea.

Cappuccino: one-third espresso, one-third steamed milk and one-third frothed milk. A traditional Italian cappuccino is 4.5oz, but in the UK they are usually larger. Often topped with powdered chocolate or cinnamon.

Cherry: a term used to refer to the fruit of the coffee plant, each of which usually contains two coffee beans.

Cortado: a traditional Spanish coffee made with a shot of espresso and a dash of warm milk to reduce acidity.

Crema: the pale brown foam on the surface of an espresso, created by the dispersion of gases in liquid at high pressure. A sign of a well-extracted shot.

Cupping: a method by which professional tasters perform sensory evaluation of coffee beans. Water is poured over ground beans and the coffee is left to stand for a few minutes to allow extraction. The taster smells the coffee, then slurps it from a spoon or directly from the cup. The grounds remain within the liquid, so tasters often spit it out after allowing the flavour, body and acidity to register in the mouth.

Dispersion screen: an essential part of the brew group that ensures the correct dispersion of brewing water over the portafilter and filter basket.

Dosage: the amount of ground coffee used for each brewing method. For espresso, dosage should be 7g per 1.5oz shot.

Doppio: a double espresso, or three to six ounces of straight espresso.

Drip or filter method: a brewing method that allows hot water to settle through a bed of ground coffee, either with or without a filter paper.

Espresso: the basis for the majority of coffee beverages in coffee shops, made by forcing hot water at high pressure through 7g of finely ground coffee to produce 1.5oz of extracted beverage.

Extraction: the act of turning water into brewed coffee or espresso by allowing coffee to sit in hot water for a period of time or forcing hot water through ground coffee.

Filter basket: sits in the portafilter and holds a bed of ground coffee. The basket has a multitude of tiny holes in the bottom to allow the extracted beverage to seep through and pour into a cup.

Coffee Glossary cont.

Filter method: any brewing method in which water filters through a bed of ground coffee. Most commonly used to describe drip method brewers that use a paper filter to separate grounds from brewed coffee.

Flat white: an espresso-based beverage hailing from Australia and New Zealand made with a double shot of espresso and finely steamed milk (or microfoam). Typically served as an 8oz drink, a flat white is similar to a traditional Italian cappuccino and is often served with latte art.

Flavour: one of the principal categories used by professional tasters to determine the quality of a coffee or blend. Flavour refers to the taste and notes such as citrus, nutty, earthy and exotic, which describe the coffee.

French press, plunger pot, cafétiere: brewing method that separates spent grounds from brewed coffee by pressing them to the bottom of the brewing receptacle with a mesh plunger.

Froth / foam: as milk is steamed using a steaming wand, air is introduced into the liquid, resulting in the production of froth. As the steam agitates and heats the milk, it increases in volume and the wand tip is moved towards the surface. This draws air at high velocity into the milk, creating the foam or froth. Steamed milk and froth should be poured, not spooned, into the cup.

Green coffee (green beans): unroasted coffee.

Grind: the extent to which whole coffee beans are ground, a factor that will play a significant role in determining the resulting coffee brewed from it. A coarse grind should be used for a brewing method where the grounds will sit in the water for a period of time. A very fine grind is suited to high-speed brewing or extraction methods such as espresso.

Grouphead: the part of the brew group containing the locking connector for the portafilter and the dispersion screen. An integral part of the espresso machine, the grouphead helps to maintain temperature stability in the machine, essential for producing a perfect shot.

Latte or caffè latte: a shot of espresso combined with about three times as much hot milk, topped with foamed milk.

Latte art: the pattern or design created by pouring steamed milk into a shot of espresso. Only properly steamed milk will hold its form, and latte art is a good sign of a skilled barista.

Long black: made by pulling a double shot of espresso over hot water. Similar to an Americano, but different in that it retains the crema from the espresso and has a stronger flavour.

Macchiato: a serving of espresso "stained" with a small quantity of hot frothed milk (espresso macchiato) or a moderately tall (8oz) glass of hot frothed milk "stained" with espresso (latte macchiato).

Macrofoam or dry foam: the stiff foam containing large bubbles that is created when steaming milk for a cappuccino.

Microfoam: the ideal texture of steamed milk for espresso-based coffee drinks, particularly those with latte art. Microfoam is made using a steam wand on an espresso machine and typically has much smaller bubbles than macrofoam.

Moka pot or stovetop: a manual method of making strong coffee. Often brewed on a stove, this type of coffee pot forces hot water through a bed of coffee using the pressure of steam and produces a strong, condensed shot of coffee.

Over extracted: a term used to describe coffee with a bitter or burnt taste, usually the result of exposing hot water to ground coffee for too long. To make the perfect coffee, water should be introduced for a set amount of time, depending on how coarsely or finely the coffee beans have been ground.

Percolation: any method of coffee brewing in which hot water percolates or filters down through a bed of ground coffee. The pumping percolator utilises the power of boiling water to force water up a tube and over a bed of ground coffee.

Piccolo: a version of a caffè latte served in a macchiato glass consisting of a shot of espresso topped with milk and foam.

Pod: a self-contained, pre-ground, pre-pressed puck of ground coffee, usually sold individually wrapped inside a perforated paper filter. The pod is used in a specific type of coffee machine and is designed for ease of use.

Pourover: a method of drip coffee in which a thin, steady stream of water is poured slowly over a filter cone filled with ground coffee.

Portafilter (groupo): the device that combines a filter basket and a handle that is designed to be quickly attached to an espresso machine. Water is forced through the portafilter and espresso pours from the spout underneath.

Coffee Glossary cont.

Puck: after a shot of espresso has been brewed, the bed of coffee grounds forms a hard, compressed object that resembles a hockey puck. Also referred to as a spent puck.

Red eye: a shot of espresso fortified with drip coffee.

Ristretto: a restricted shot made using the same dose of ground coffee as a double espresso, but with only about 1.5oz (or less) of water, poured in the normal brewing time of 25-30 seconds. The result is a richer and more intense beverage.

Roast: the method by which green coffee is heated in order to produce coffee beans for consumption. Roasting begins when the temperature inside the green bean reaches approximately 200°C (this varies between different varieties of beans). Caramelisation occurs as intense heat converts starches in the bean to simple sugars that begin to brown, giving the coffee bean a resulting brown colour.

Robusta, Coffea canephora: the next most cultivated coffee species after Coffea arabica, robusta produces about 30% of the world's coffee. Robusta is grown at lower altitudes than arabica and is a hardy, robust plant that can produce high yields. The flavour is often less refined and robusta has a much higher caffeine content than arabica.

Shot: a single unit of brewed espresso.

Single origin: coffee from a particular region or farm.

Steam wand: the visible external pipe found on most espresso machines that is used to froth and steam milk.

Syphon: a brewing method that uses two glass chambers and a direct heat source to create a fragrant, delicately flavoured cup of coffee.

Tamp (tamping): the act of pressing and compacting a bed of loose ground coffee into the portafilter basket in preparation for brewing espresso. The harder the coffee is tamped, the tighter the puck and the harder it is to extract the coffee. If the coffee grounds are too loosely tamped, the water will flow through too quickly.

Under extracted: describes coffee that has not been exposed to water for long enough. The resulting brew is often weak and thin-bodied.

Whole bean coffee: coffee that has been roasted but not yet ground.

A-Z List of Coffee Venues

3 Little Pigs at Black Truffle Warren St p80

Allpress Espresso Roastery p90

Artisan p140

Bar Italia p28

Barossa p141

Bea's of Bloomsbury Theobald's Road p60

Betty's Coffee p102

Birdhouse p142

Black Lab Coffee House, The p144

Borough Barista, The p4

Brew p145

Brick Lane Coffee p92

Browns of Brockley p128

Cà Phê VN p103

Caffè Nero Bedford Street p5

Ca'puccino p152

Caravan p48

Climpson & Sons p104

Coco di Mama p49

Coffee Circus p61

Coffee Plant p153

Coleman Coffee p81

Container Café, The p106

Costa Coffee Great Portland Street p6

Counter Café, The p107

Dark Fluid p81

Department of Coffee & Social Affairs p50

Deptford Project, The p130

Dose Espresso p51

E5 Bakehouse p108

Esoteria p109

Espresso Room, The p62

Fabrica p110

Farm Collective p52

Federation Coffee p146

Fernandez & Wells Beak Street p30

Fernandez & Wells Somerset House p7

Fix 126 p93

Fix p64

Flat Cap Coffee Co p82

Flat White p32

Fleet River Bakery p65

Foxcroft & Ginger p34

Fred & Fran p111

Full Stop Bar p94

Gail's Queen's Park p154

Get Coffee p53

Giddy Up p82

Ginger & White p66

Grind Coffee Bar Westfield Stratford p112

Grind Coffee Bar Putney p147

Hackney Pearl, The p113

Joe & the Juice Regent Street p8

Kaffeine p10

Kipferl p67

Ladurée Harrods p155

Lanka p68

Lantana p12

Le Pain Quotidien Parsons Green p148

Leila's p95

Lemon Monkey p114

Leyas p69

A-Z List of Coffee Venues cont.

Look Mum No Hands! p70
Maison d'Etre p72
Melrose & Morgan Primrose Hill p73
Merito Coffee p83
Milkbar p35
Monmouth Coffee Company Covent Garden p14
Monmouth Coffee Company The Borough p132
Mouse & De Lotz p115
New Row Coffee p15
Nomad Espresso p83
Nordic Bakery p36
Notes, Music & Coffee Wellington Street p16
Nude Espresso Hanbury Street p96
Nude Espresso Soho Square p38
Ottolenghi Islington p74
Pacific Social Club p116
Patisserie Valerie Marylebone p17
Pavilion p117
Pitch 42 at Whitecross Street Market p85
Princi p40
Providores & Tapa Room, The p18
Prufrock Coffee at Present p84
Prufrock Coffee Leather Lane p54
Railroad p118
Reilly Rocket p120
Reynolds Charlotte Street p19
Roastery (Bullet Coffee Cartel), The p149
Sacred Ganton Street p41
Sacred Highbury Studios p76
Sandwich & the Spoon, The p85
ScooterCaffè p134
Sensory Lab p20
Shoreditch Grind p98
Speakeasy p42
St. David Coffee House p135
St. Ali p56
Starbucks Conduit Street p44
Store Street Espresso p22
Tapped & Packed Rathbone Place p25
Tapped & Packed Tottenham Court Road p24
Taylor St Baristas Canary Wharf p136
Taylor St Baristas Old Broad Street p99
Tina, We Salute You p122
Tinderbox p78
Tomtom Coffee House p156
Towpath p123
Wild & Wood Coffee p79
Wilton Way Café p124

Coffee Map Key

West End

1 **The Borough Barista** p4
2 **Caffè Nero** Bedford Street p5
3 **Costa Coffee** Great Portland Street p6
4 **Fernandez & Wells** Somerset House p7
5 **Joe & the Juice** Regent Street p8
TOP30 6 **Kaffeine** p10
TOP30 7 **Lantana** p12
TOP30 8 **Monmouth Coffee Company** Covent Garden p14
9 **New Row Coffee** p15
TOP30 10 **Notes, Music & Coffee** Wellington Street p16
11 **Patisserie Valerie** Marylebone p17
12 **The Providores & Tapa Room** p18
13 **Reynolds** Charlotte Street p19
TOP30 14 **Sensory Lab** p20
TOP30 15 **Store Street Espresso** p22
TOP30 16 **Tapped & Packed** Rathbone Place p24
17 **Tapped & Packed** Tottenham Court Road p25

Soho

18 **Bar Italia** p28
TOP30 19 **Fernandez & Wells** Beak Street p30
TOP30 20 **Flat White** p32
21 **Foxcroft & Ginger** p34
TOP30 22 **Milkbar** p35
23 **Nordic Bakery** p36
24 **Nude Espresso** Soho Square p38
25 **Princi** p40
TOP30 26 **Sacred** Ganton Street p41
TOP30 27 **Speakeasy** p42
28 **Starbucks** Conduit Street p44

Farringdon & Clerkenwell

TOP30 29 **Caravan** p48
30 **Coco di Mama** p49
31 **Department of Coffee & Social Affairs** p50
TOP30 32 **Dose Espresso** p51
33 **Farm Collective** p52
34 **Get Coffee** p53
TOP30 35 **Prufrock Coffee** Leather Lane p54
TOP30 36 **St. Ali** p56

Camden & Islington

37 **Bea's of Bloomsbury** Theobald's Road p60
38 **Coffee Circus** Crouch Hill p61
TOP30 39 **The Espresso Room** p62
40 **Fix** Whitecross Street p64
41 **Fleet River Bakery** p65
42 **Ginger & White** p66
43 **Kipferl** p67
44 **Lanka** p68
45 **Leyas** p69
TOP30 46 **Look Mum No Hands!** p70
47 **Maison d'Etre** p72
48 **Melrose & Morgan** Primrose Hill p73
TOP30 49 **Ottolenghi** Islington p74
50 **Sacred** Highbury Studios p76
51 **Tinderbox** p78
52 **Wild & Wood Coffee** p79

Inner East

TOP30 53 **Allpress Espresso Roastery** p90
54 **Brick Lane Coffee** p92
55 **Fix 126** p93
56 **Full Stop** p94
57 **Leila's** p95
TOP30 58 **Nude Espresso** Hanbury Street p96
59 **Shoreditch Grind** p98
60 **Taylor St Baristas** Old Broad Street p99

Hackney

61 **Betty's Coffee** p102
62 **Cà Phê VN** Broadway Market p103
TOP30 63 **Climpson & Sons** p104
64 **The Container Café** p106
TOP30 65 **The Counter Café** p107
66 **E5 Bakehouse** p108
67 **Esoteria** p109
TOP30 68 **Fabrica** p110
69 **Fred & Fran** p111
70 **Grind Coffee Bar** Westfield Stratford p112
71 **The Hackney Pearl** p113
72 **Lemon Monkey** p114
73 **Mouse & De Lotz** p115
74 **Pacific Social Club** p116
75 **Pavilion** p117
76 **Railroad** p118
77 **Reilly Rocket** p120
TOP30 78 **Tina, We Salute You** p122
79 **Towpath** p123
TOP30 80 **Wilton Way Café** p124

South East London

TOP30 81 **Browns of Brockley** p128
82 **The Deptford Project** p130
TOP30 83 **Monmouth Coffee Company** The Borough p132
84 **ScooterCaffè** p134
85 **St. David Coffee House** p135
TOP30 86 **Taylor St Baristas** Canary Wharf p136

South West London

87 **Artisan** p140
88 **Barossa** p141
89 **Birdhouse** p142
TOP30 90 **The Black Lab Coffee House** p144
91 **Brew** p145
92 **Federation Coffee** p146
93 **Grind Coffee Bar** Putney p147
94 **Le Pain Quotidien** Parsons Green p148
95 **The Roastery (Bullet Coffee Cartel)** p149

West London

96 **Ca'puccino** p152
97 **Coffee Plant** p153
98 **Gail's** Queen's Park p154
99 **Ladurée** Harrods p155
100 **Tomtom Coffee House** p156

Carts, Stalls & Kiosks

A **3 Little Pigs** at Black Truffle Warren Street p80
B **Coleman Coffee** p81
C **Dark Fluid** at Brockley Market p81
D **Flat Cap Coffee Co** p82
E **Giddy Up** p82
F **Merito Coffee** p83
G **Nomad Espresso** p83
H **Pitch 42 at Whitecross Street Market** p85
I **Prufrock Coffee** at Present p84
J **The Sandwich & the Spoon** p85